The Purposes and the Performance of Higher Education in the United States

APPROACHING THE YEAR 2000

A Report and Recommendations by
The Carnegie Commission on Higher Education

JUNE 1973

MCGRAW-HILL BOOK COMPANY
New York   St. Louis   San Francisco   Düsseldorf
London   Sydney   Toronto   Mexico   Panama
Johannesburg   Kuala Lumpur   Montreal
New Delhi   Sao Paulo   Singapore

This report is issued by the Carnegie Commission on
Higher Education, with headquarters at
1947 Center Street, Berkeley, California 94704.
The views and conclusions expressed in this report
are solely those of the members of the Carnegie Commission
on Higher Education and do not necessarily reflect the
views or opinions of the Carnegie Corporation of New York,
The Carnegie Foundation for the Advancement of Teaching,
or their trustees, officers, directors, or employees.

Library of Congress Cataloging in Publication Data

Carnegie Commission on Higher Education
The purposes and the performance of higher education in the United States:
Approaching the year 2000.
"The Carnegie Commission on Higher Education series"
1. Education, Higher—United States. 2. Education,
Higher—Aims and objectives. I. Title.
II. Title: Approaching the year 2000. III. Series
LA227.3.C375   378'.01'0973   73-8674
ISBN 0-07-010071-3

Additional copies of this report may be ordered from
McGraw-Hill Book Company, Hightstown, New Jersey 08520.
The price is $2.45 a copy.

'To every thing there is a season, and a time to every purpose under the heaven.'

ECCLESIASTES

Contents

NOTE: A technical report presenting data related to chapters 3, 4, 5 and 6 will be printed separately and will be available directly from the Carnegie Commission on Higher Education. It will be entitled *Technical Notes on Purposes and Performance in Higher Education.*

Foreword

This report is concerned with the purposes and the performance of higher education in the United States.

Purposes have grown quantitatively and changed substantially qualitatively in the course of American history but have not been decisively reordered since the period around 1870. At that time higher education—reflecting new purposes—greatly expanded its functions to include research and service to society, and opened its doors potentially to the mass entry of students. Another major review of purposes is now taking place, although it does not appear that changes as fundamental as those of a century ago will now occur. However, purposes can no longer be so taken for granted, so assumed as correctly embodied in current practice, as they have been for much of the past century.

We define purposes as being the intentions of higher education, as constituting the general design of higher education, as comprising the end objects it pursues. We define functions as the specific acts performed in the course of fulfilling the purposes. Some of these functions are (1) directly related to the purposes, such as teaching; others are (2) support functions only indirectly related to purposes, such as conduct of business affairs; and others are (3) ancillary functions, such as the conduct of governmental laboratories. Functions are actions that serve, directly or indirectly, as a means to carry out a purpose or purposes. Purposes are intenional, and functions are instrumental. Beyond both purposes and functions lie means of accomplishment such as freedom, money, and personnel.

It is customary to say that higher education has three "purposes": teaching, research, and service. These are more instrumental functions or means, as we define them, and less intentional purposes or ultimate ends; whichever way they are viewed, they require amplification. But the discussion of purposes needs to go beyond the standard reference to the classical triad.

Nonmarket institutions—which colleges largely are—need to give more careful consideration to a definition of their goals than do market institutions which have one major goal—satisfying the market at a profit, leaving ultimate "purposes" to the consumers.

In this report, we set forth five major purposes for higher education in the United States, as we see them, in the last quarter of the twentieth century. Purposes guide the specific functions performed, which in turn, affect the nature of governance and the methods of financing. Thus purposes reach far into the conduct of higher education.

We also seek to comment upon the performance of higher education in the United States; to evaluate how well or how poorly it has fulfilled its purposes; to indicate its accomplishments and its failures; and to make suggestions for improvements.

We also raise the question of whether higher education in general or individual institutions specifically are now seeking to perform too many functions; whether an overloading of functions should be a major source of concern. The purposes of all of higher education do have an impact on the functions of individual institutions, but it is in no way suggested that all institutions should be involved with all purposes; quite the contrary. We favor differentiation of functions among institutions even as we set forth the purposes for higher education more broadly than we do for a single institution.

Conflicting schools of thought about primary purposes have contended over the centuries. We draw them together for expository purposes under three broad headings and seek to set forth their respective inherent characters. We believe, however, that theoretical doctrines, while influential, are not solely controlling. They have their impacts within the context of the surrounding society. This context has been changing substantially as the surrounding society has changed. Some degree of consistency inevitably exists between American society and the subsystem of higher education that operates within it. Thus purposes must be viewed both in relation to philosophical orientations and to the nature of and changes in society. The contending theories—contending as much or more than ever before—and the changing relations with society both portend, we believe, a continuing conflict over purposes.

The effective resolution of this current contest over purposes, nevertheless, is crucial both to the internal health and to the external support of higher education. We make suggestions as to how we believe this crisis of purposes can best be guided.

We have drawn, in particular, on the following commentaries on higher education in the United States prepared for the Commission by scholars from abroad who are well informed about our affairs: *Any Person, Any Study* by Eric Ashby (McGraw-Hill, 1971); *American Higher Education* by Joseph Ben-David (McGraw-Hill, 1971); *The Academic System in American Society* by Alain Touraine (forthcoming); and *Some Dilemmas in Higher Education Today* by Michio Nagai (forthcoming). Other reports prepared for the Commission that have been particularly helpful include *The American College and the American Culture* by Oscar and Mary F. Handlin (McGraw-Hill, 1970); *Recent Alumni and Higher Education* by Joe L. Spaeth and Andrew M. Greeley (McGraw-Hill, 1970); *Institutions in Transition* by Harold Hodgkinson (McGraw-Hill, 1971); *A Degree and What Else?* by Stephen B. Withey (McGraw-Hill, 1971); *The Home of Science* by Dael Wolfle (McGraw-Hill, 1972); *The University as an Organization* edited by James A. Perkins (McGraw-Hill, 1973); *Academic Transformation* edited by David Riesman and Verne A. Stadtman (forthcoming); *Content and Context* edited by Carl Kaysen (forthcoming); *The Beginning of the Future: A Historical Approach to Graduate Education in the Arts and Sciences* by Richard Storr (forthcoming); *The Rise of the Arts* by Jack Morrison (forthcoming); *Education, Income, and Human Behavior* (tentative title) edited by F. Thomas Juster (forthcoming). We have also made use of information from the Carnegie Commission Survey of Faculty and Student Opinion conducted by Martin Trow and Joseph Zelan.

We express appreciation to members of the staff for assistance in the preparation of this report. Technical notes on the Education of the Individual Student and the Provision of a Constructive Environment for Developmental Growth, Advancing Human Capability in Society at Large, Educational Justice for the Postsecondary Age Group, Pure Learning—Supporting Intellectual and Artistic Creativity will be published separately and will be available from the Carnegie Commission on Higher Education in a document entitled *Technical Notes on Purposes and Performance in Higher Education.*

*The Purposes
and the Performance
of Higher Education
in the United States*

1. Major Themes

1 Conflicts over purposes exist in higher education in the United States today. These conflicts affect both internal conduct of institutions and external relations between institutions and society. A period for reexamination of purposes somewhat comparable to—but less intense than—that of a century ago is at hand.

2 The main purposes of higher education in the United States today, and for the prospective future, as we see them, are:

- The provision of opportunities for the intellectual, aesthetic, ethical, and skill development of individual students, and the provision of campus environments which can constructively assist students in their more general developmental growth

- The advancement of human capability in society at large

- The enlargement of educational justice for the postsecondary age group

- The transmission and advancement of learning and wisdom

- The critical evaluation of society—through individual thought and persuasion—for the sake of society's self-renewal

These are purposes for the whole system of higher education. Individual institutions will relate more to some than to others. Neither the purposes as envisioned nor performance related to them apply equally to all institutions.

3 We rate the actual performance of the first of these purposes as generally adequate; the second, as superior; the third, as unsatisfactory but improving; the fourth, as superior; and the fifth, as quite uneven in the past and uncertain for the future.

4   We suggest improvements particularly as follows:

First purpose

More attention to the general education of students, to the opportunities for their occupational preparation, and to the enhancement of their creative abilities

More concern for the quality of the environment which affects the developmental growth of students; in particular, more mixing of studies with work and service, and more mixing of age groups on campus

Second purpose

A steadier supply of federal research funds, particularly for basic research, and concentrated on the most productive individuals and projects

A major effort to reduce deficits in the health manpower field by the end of this decade

A major expansion of opportunities for "life-long learning"

Third purpose

A determined effort to provide places in college for young persons who wish to attend from low-income and minority groups, with adequate financial assistance for their support and with respect for their cultural backgrounds

A greater concern for the opportunities available to the total postsecondary age group, and for the total contribution of postsecondary education to the achievement of social justice

Fourth purpose

More research support for the humanities, the social sciences, and the creative arts, along with steadier support for the sciences

Fifth purpose

Better rules and understandings to govern exercise of the critical evaluation of society

Better appreciation by the public of the importance of this activity

5   Actual purposes assigned to higher education and the functions related to them have accumulated over the three centuries since the founding of Harvard. Higher education in America started with an emphasis on training in the classical culture and the moral precepts of the day. It added attention to economic growth, to the development of a democratic policy, and to service to society generally. The functions now performed are both substantial and complex.

6 Higher education is now heavily loaded with functions. At least one of these functions is a contradiction against the inherent nature of academic life. A few are ineffectively or unwisely performed by the campus itself. Still others are inconsistently combined with each other within individual institutions. We propose a search for greater cohesion.

7 Three major doctrinal views about central purpose are found within higher education: (1) that it should be concerned with a search for and a socialization to values, (2) that it should serve the cause of the continuing evolution of knowledge and of skill development within existing society, and (3) that it should help prepare the way for (or assist the perpetuation of) some designated type of society. The first of these views was supreme in the United States before the Civil War. The second has been dominant for the past century. The third view now constitutes the main challenge to the still dominant approach. Conflict over these doctrines has recently become more active. Purposes actually served and functions actually performed do reflect doctrinal considerations, but, more particularly, they reflect the nature and the needs of the surrounding society. Doctrinal disagreement takes place within the context of the surrounding social relationships.

8 A continuing conflict over purposes must be expected in the future resulting, most likely, in the end, in a continuation of the currently ascendent approach but subject to some substantial modifications. The conflict, however, may, in the meantime, be quite intense although intermittent in the level of its intensity. We believe that both higher education and American society should be alert to the possibility of a "time of troubles" over purposes, should understand that the "good old days" of consensus over purposes may not soon return, and should realize that a "political dissensus" now exists on campus which has major implications for recurrent con-

frontations on campus and with society over the fundamental logic of the academic endeavor.

9 Many of the highly controversial individual issues relative to purposes are now before higher education that reflect the more fundamental doctrinal views about purposes but which are important in their own right:

Should there be a concern for the student *as a total person,* now that the old policy of *in loco parentis* has been abandoned and, if so, how should it be expressed?

Should *special consideration* be given to members of minority groups and to women in admissions of students and in employment of faculty members in order to rectify historical and present imbalances? Should quotas be established? Should a lottery system be invoked?

Is there now an *unfair discrimination in favor of the college attender* as against those who do not attend college?

Should higher education seek to further *equality of opportunity* with differentiated results *or a flat equality of results* in terms of grades and degrees regardless of ability and effort?

Should organized faculties, as corporate bodies, *take positions on political controversies* not directly related to the welfare of the campus?

Should the campus become an important *base for promoting a new type of society* for the future against the majority wishes of the surrounding society?

These are among the specific issues in debate and which we discuss. The battles over them will often be impassioned.

10 Higher education and American society have a common interest in working out purposeful mutual relationships as each shapes and, in turn, is shaped by the other. Fortunately, higher education in the United States has demonstrated a degree of adaptability to changed circumstances which distinguishes it from some other more rigid national systems that respond only to governmental direction in emergency situations. Fortunately, also, American society has demonstrated substantial support for and tolerance of a major degree of independence by higher education, although these may now be diminishing.

11 The campus is a place for concern with values, but it is not a church; for concern with public policy issues, but it is not a political party; for concern with the environment for the developmental growth of students, but it is not a parent; for concern with effective management of its own affairs, but it is not in business to manage the affairs of others; for concern with the application of the coercive power of government, but it has neither the power nor the responsibility of government; for concern with the physical conditions of life of its members, but it should not be a "company town." Some persons seek to make the campus, in part, into a church or a political party or a substitute parent or a business management enterprise or an alternative government or a "company town," but these are not the roles the campus either should play or can play effectively.

The campus is above all a center for learning in what is, in the phrase of Hutchins (1968), increasingly a "Learning Society." It is the preeminent place for the giving and receiving of instruction at high levels to all who want it and can benefit from it, and for acquiring knowledge through research and reflection and making it available to any and all who have an interest in it. "The pursuit of truth and learning is the central value of the university" (Committee on Governance, Harvard University, 1971).

12 Higher education serves more than one purpose. It is thus subject to more than one test of performance.

The several purposes served are essential to society. They have generally been adequately fulfilled, although not equally satisfactorily in each area of performance.

One central reason for the generally adequate level of performance is that institutes of higher education in the United States are marked both by diversity among them and by competition between them. Preservation of this differentiation of functions and styles, and this competitive spirit is, consequently, of great importance.

Part One:
Purposes and Performance

2. Forces for a Reevaluation of Purposes

One century ago, the United States was undergoing great change and so also was higher education within it. The Civil War was over and the principle of maintaining the United States as a single nation had been reaffirmed. The West was yielding to agriculture, and industrialization was spreading throughout the North and East. New immigrant groups began arriving in large numbers. It was a period of national resurgence, of economic expansion, of political populism. The "classical" college devoted to *in loco parentis,* to the Bible, and to European culture gave way to the "modern" college and university open to scientific research, to training for new professions and occupations, to service to society, to a more welcoming approach to students from all income strata. Forces which began building about 1820 reached a climax between 1870 and 1890, and had worked a great transformation by the time of World War I. The new model of higher education which resulted was largely unchallenged, except for rear-guard efforts, until very recent times.

Once again, great—but mostly quite different—forces are at work, including:

- A further extension of educational opportunity to members of minority groups, to women, and to adults. Higher education has moved from its elite stage to its mass stage, and is now moving to the stage of universal access. This has many impacts on total numbers, on the size of institutions and their consequent lesser sense of community, on the interests of the students—more technical and less strictly academic—and on labor market opportunities for those who have attended college. The revolution of rising expectations for access to higher education is now reaching its final climax.

- New knowledge is more central to the conduct of society. It has taken its place along with land, labor, capital, and management as a great factor influencing production. It is also more basic to the conduct of public affairs and to the daily lives of individuals. And higher education is the focal point for the creation of new knowledge. Thus higher education is of more interest to more institutions within society than it once was, and is more entwined with them, including the "military-industrial complex." It is also of more interest to more individuals.

- Intellectuals, trained within higher education and often clustered around it, are both more numerous within society and more essential to its performance. They follow, however, many points of view, including support of the "adversary culture." A new social struggle of some intellectuals against the status quo marks every advanced industrial nation, including the United States. Higher education is inevitably affected by this confrontation. The older struggle in the factory of workers versus capitalists over shares of the product is giving way in its social significance to the newer struggle on the campus and in the media of some intellectuals versus many other citizens over the rate and the directions of social change.

- Society is in the process of reexamining values and life styles, with the campus heavily involved in the process of this examination. New mentalities may be in the process of being born as they were during the Renaissance, the Reformation, and the American and French Revolutions. Debates over national views as against international considerations, over the comparative emphasis on competition in production as against equality in consumption, and over the respective roles of the individual and the state mark some of the great issues in contention.

- Students are changing. They come out of more permissive environments. They are more oriented in college toward their developmental process in its totality. Many of them are more activist toward conditions on the campus and toward the societal environments within which they find themselves. They are less willing to be "socialized" into standard patterns set by others.

These are among the forces that require a new look at the purposes and functions of higher education. It is no longer sufficient to say that higher education has the purposes of "teaching, research, and service." Teaching to what ends? Research for what reasons? Service to whom?

We are particularly concerned with purposes for this time—the last quarter of the twentieth century—and for this place—the United States—while recognizing that some purposes of higher education should be both universal and eternal.

We next set forth the five major purposes toward which we believe that higher education in the United States should now be directed, our evaluation of the performance of higher education in each of these areas, and our suggestions for improvements.

3. Purpose 1: The Education of the Individual Student and the Provision of a Constructive Environment for Developmental Growth

Nine million students are now on campus. The years in college are both an important segment of their lives and a unique opportunity to affect all of the rest of their lives—students frequently have a greater chance to determine the course of their lives through their own choices while they are in college than at any earlier or later time in life. It is a period of unusually free choice for them in their development.

The campus can aid the development of students in several ways by providing opportunities for:

Acquiring a general understanding of society and of the place of the individual within it—this is the role of "general" education and it includes contact with history and with the nature of other cultures

Making a choice among diverse intellectual environments so that the student has a better chance of finding one that matches his or her interests and talents

Developing a "critical" mind in the sense of the capacity to "test and challenge . . . previously unexamined assumptions" (Keniston & Gerzon, 1971) and also unexamined new ideas

Training that will aid in obtaining suitable employment

Surveying and intensifying cultural and creative interests to enrich life; enhancing the expressive as well as the verbal and mathematical talents

Studying ethical issues, and forming values and life goals

Working out problems in connection with their "emotional growth"

Meeting with and working with diverse types of people, and thus "learning to get along with people"

Participating in extracurricular activities that give outlet to athletic, artistic, and other out-of-course interests

Participating in work and service activity that provides contacts with other aspects of society, and experience in using skills and exercising responsibility—this may require stopping out and stopping in

Trying out many interests and possible talents, and even failing at some without heavy consequences

Gaining access to advice and counsel from professional experts and from qualified adults in the campus community on both a formal and informal basis

Our Carnegie Commission Survey of Faculty and Student Opinion indicates some of the priorities that undergraduate students place on several of these opportunities, but it should be noted that the results we obtained are the prisoners of the specific questions asked. From this set of data, however, it would appear that undergraduate students themselves place a particularly high priority on the following and in this general order:

Their "emotional growth"

"Learning to get along with people"

"Formation of values and goals"

"A detailed grasp of a special field"

"A well-rounded general education"

"Training and skills for an occupation"

"Outlets for creative activities"

"Earning power"

When they were questioned about their evaluation of results in each of these areas, the students generally reported that they received "much" or "some" of what they wanted. The lowest rating was in occupational training. No question about results was asked in connection with "emotional growth," which ranks at the top of the above list, and students, of course, do not yet know what their additional earning power will be. (For the statistical data on which the above comments are based, see Table 1.) Related, but unfor-

TABLE 1 *Aspirations and attainments of undergraduates*

Goal	Consider essential (percent)	Consider essential and received		
		None (percent)	Some (percent)	Much (percent)
Learning to get along with people	77	7	36	57
Formation of values and goals of my life	72	13	51	36
Detailed grasp of a special field	62	8	56	36
Well-rounded general education	57	2	52	46
Training and skills for an occupation	57	15	53	32
	"Strongly agree" or "agree with reservations" (percent)			
Undergraduate education in America should be improved if:				
More attention were paid to the emotional growth of students	83			
The chief benefit of a college education that it increases one's earning power	48			
	Responding "not enough" (percent)			
All in all, in terms of your own needs and desires, how much of the following have you had:				
Outlets for creative activities	55			

SOURCE: Carnegie Commission Survey of Faculty and Student Opinion.

tunately not comparable, data on graduate students are shown in Table 2. "Growth" appears, for example, to be less important, and "earning power" more important for graduate students.

The reactions of undergraduates indicate that they view the college experience as one related to their total developmental growth, and not to the cognitive and occupational aspects of their lives alone. They thus expect more out of their college experience than the college, *as an institution,* often can and even should deliver, particularly in the area of personal development. They generally, in harsh fact, expect the most where the college as an institution can deliver the least; but students may have an opportunity to meet their goals through their own efforts within the college en-

	"Strongly agree' or "agree with reservations"
TABLE 2 Aspirations of graduate students Goal	(percent)
Continue my intellectual growth	96
Increase my earning power	84
Better serve mankind	76
Prepare for an academic career	68
Satisfy job requirements	66
Obtain an occupation with high prestige	60
Contribute to my ability to change society	60
Get a teaching credential	39
Find myself	27
Engage in political activities	12

SOURCE: Carnegie Commission Survey of Faculty and Student Opinion.

vironment better than they can in some of the alternative environments available to them. Thus the college experience provides
more opportunities for them than does the college itself.

Two questions thus arise: What should the college make available by way of direct opportunities? And what kind of environment
can the college help to provide which will assist students to attain
those personal goals for which the college has no direct responsibility?

A broader developmental approach to the college experience,
going beyond intellectual development alone, is in keeping with
new insights in the field of psychology, as, for example, in the writings of Erik Erikson—the college years are an important developmental period, and cognitive and affective activities are closely
related to each other. Yet the campus cannot and should not try to
take direct responsibility for the "total" development of the student. That responsibility belongs primarily to the individual student
by the time he goes to college. The primary direct responsibility of the college is to assist with intellectual and skill development, and to a lesser extent with aesthetic and ethical development
also, through teaching and through college-related activities. The
college, however, also does provide an important environment
composed of the faculty members recruited, the fellow students
admitted, the coaches and counselors hired, the cultural programs

provided, the service opportunities offered, the traditions and rules in effect, and other elements. But it is only one of the several environments within which the student lives; other environments are provided by the family, the church, the communications media, jobs, and by other aspects of society. Also, developmental growth can take place in many environments and, for some, the college campus may not by any means be the ideal place. The college, however, is the preeminent place for developing intellectual discipline and scholarly and professional competence. Thus the college should particularly devote its attention to what it can do best and to what students cannot so well obtain anywhere else. The campus is, above all, a place where students can enrich their minds by study. "Totalism" in the campus approach to students, we believe, is neither wise nor possible.

Thus, the college cannot assume the full developmental responsibility for students. Nor do we believe that it should—to do so it would need to try to "play God" for the students, which is repugnant to democratic principles. No one institution of higher education should take unto itself the total domination of the individual personality. There is no single model of the preferred total personality as there was of the "Victorian Gentleman" (Wilkinson, 1964); if there were, it would still be questionable whether higher education should seek to enforce it. If higher education did try, it is doubtful that it could be successful. If it succeeded, it is certain that this could lead to quite static and elitist results. Thus we by no means go as far as the statement of purpose in *Learning to Be:* "The physical, intellectual, emotional and ethical integration of the individual into a complete man is a broad definition of the fundamental aim for education" (Faure, 1972).

Consequently, the campus must seek to provide effective opportunities in the classroom and a "constructive" campus environment—in the absence of a "constructive" environment there can be a tragic loss of talent and impairment of life chances for individual students. But it must not seek to fulfill the responsibility for the total development of its students. Providing opportunities for an effective education, and determining the attributes of and providing for a "constructive" campus environment are appropriate and also sufficient tasks.

We believe that the campus has a fundamental educational development responsibility in these areas:

General education, including "an understanding of what it means to be self-governing citizen of a self-governing political community" (Hutchi 1972, p. 223)

Depth training in some special field, including occupational training

Establishment of high standards of academic conduct

Provision of access to adult members of the campus community and professional experts for advice and counsel and example

Provision of a stimulating cultural life for students

Provision of work and service opportunities

It should be possible for a student to construct for himself, out these basic campus provisions, the following:

Essential academic skills

Competency to choose and then to enter a career

Basic capacity to perform his citizenship responsibilities

Creative interests and capacities

He or she may also be aided by the general campus environment developing an overall ethical orientation, competency in soc situations, and a sense of identity, of autonomy, of personal inte rity—but these would clearly be by-products of the environme not direct campus responsibilities.

We recognize the difficulties of drawing lines up to which t campus has an environmental responsibility and beyond which does not, and of defining a "constructive" environment. Each ty of college and campus will need to draw its own lines and ma its own definitions.

The generally new elements in the situation, however, are strong concern by many students that the campus aid their "tot development; a greater realization of the potential importance the campus itself, for better or for worse, as an environment development—greater than at any time since the demise of t classical college; and also the new perspectives on the process of individual development. The campus, nevertheless, having giv up the old *in loco parentis* should not now try to stand *in lo discipuli*. The student must carry the basic responsibility for own developmental growth.

The attitude of students on this issue of developmental grow is interesting. They have rejected the strict controls of the old *in loco parentis,* but they want to keep the protection of *in loco parentis* against interference by the outside police and the law as in political confrontations or drug "busts." They seem to want to add a new campus concern for their "emotional growth." This might be called the "new style" *in loco parentis:* protection from society when protection is wanted and assistance with "growth" when such assistance is wanted. But then their expectations of parents have also changed. Most campuses and many parents have moved away from *in loco parentis* — "old style" — and are now moving toward *in loco parentis* — "new style."

We have not used the term, or the idea, of the "socialization" of students. This concept is too static for a dynamic society, too monistic in a pluralistic society; and too ethnocentric towards the campus in a society where "socialization" takes place mostly before college and where the college, as an institution, competes with the media, the peer group, the church, and many other "socializing" institutions. We have preferred to speak, instead, of educational development. The campus does, of course, have the function of socializing the student into the patterns of academic life, but this is a much narrower concept than that of socialization as generally used.

Academic socialization includes inculcation of the virtues of hard work, of postponed gratification, of the integrity of one's personal performance, of respect for the facts, of cognitive rationality, of independence of mind, of the "recognition of differential achievement," and of the "acceptance of functionally necessary authority."[1] All these are values of high importance in a successful academic life. They may also be characteristics of worth in many other endeavors.

Definition of purpose 1

The campus has a *basic* responsibility to provide good educational opportunities for its students (1) to develop an understanding of society, (2) to obtain academic and technical competence in selected fields, (3) to fulfill appropriate standards of academic conduct, and (4) to explore cultural interests and enhance cultural skills. The campus has a *subsidiary* concern to provide constructive cam-

---

[1] For a discussion of certain of these points, see Parsons and Platt (1970).

pus environment without assuming accountability for the "emo tional growth" of students.

Performance

Performance is very hard to measure in this area given the mil lions of students, the thousands of campuses, and the several and quite imprecise criteria. We do note, however, that:

- Most students are satisfied with their college experience (Carnegie Commission on Higher Education, 1972a). However, about one half drop out before reaching the final degree for which they regis ter, and at least 5 percent are on campus against their own free will (ibid).

- Undergraduates report that they mostly get "much" or "some" of what they want from their college experiences, with the greatest gap between aspiration and achievement in the area of occupa tional training (see Table 1). We expect that students might also report a substantial gap in the area of "emotional growth" if we had comparable data.

- College graduates—and presumably, in part, because of their col lege experiences—do find their jobs better paying and more inter esting and their lives more satisfying, do participate more in com munity affairs, do exhibit more tolerance toward their fellow man and do engage more in cultural activities than do those who have not attended college. They are more effective consumers. They are generally better able to make the myriad decisions with which the modern American is faced (Spaeth & Greeley, 1970; Withey 1971; Juster, forthcoming). Higher education, overall, provides ways both to invest in future possibilities and to engage in the "pursuit of happiness" on campus and in later life.

Our own evaluation is that, in terms of providing opportunities for academic and technical competence, higher education in the United States is generally adequate and sometimes superb. For meeting standards of academic conduct, it is generally adequate For exploring cultural interests and enhancing cultural skills, it is improving but the adequacy of programs varies greatly from campus to campus. And for obtaining a good general understanding of society, it is often poor and may be deteriorating (Carnegie Com mission on Higher Education, 1972a). We accept the developmenta view of youth and the expectations of many students that the can pus will be helpful to their total developmental growth, but we share with others an uncertainty as to how this continuing development can best be assured and what role the campus should play in it. Nevertheless, we are convinced that some advantageous adjustments can be made in many existing environments even as we see the great need for more careful thought, more experiments, and more testing of the results of existing and newly experimental environments. The college environment, we believe, is often a quite artificial "hothouse," (1) too far removed from work and service, and (2) too age-stratified to youth alone. More work and service opportunities can be provided by work-study jobs on campus and off, by facilitating off-campus service work as through Brooks House at Harvard, and by encouraging part-time employment opportunities for students by outside employers and providing contact with part-time jobs more generally. We are particularly concerned that on some campuses there has been an abdication by adults of their responsibilities to advise and to guide and to serve as models, and that there has been an unhealthy rise of a spirit of "peer totalism" and of pressures for peer-group conformity that can warp individual lives.

See Note A in *Technical Notes on Purposes and Performance in Higher Education* (Carnegie Commission on Higher Education, forthcoming).

Recommendation 1: More broad learning experiences should be made available to students, and more opportunities for creative activity should be provided as through independent study and the creative arts.

Recommendation 2: More work and service opportunities should be created for students by government and industry and non-profit agencies, and students should be encouraged to pursue these opportunities, including, occasionally, through "stop-outs."

Recommendation 3: More attention should be paid to the occupational training interests of students, and to occupational counselling and guidance as students and adults seek to adjust to changing labor market conditions.

Recommendation 4: There should be a greater mixing of age groups on campus through providing more opportunities for older persons to take classes and to obtain needed financial support. We make this recommendation not only for the sake of mixing the age groups, but primarily for the sake of making these opportunities available to adults of all ages.

We see a coming problem, of perhaps substantial significance, in connection with the purpose of individual student development. That problem is how to provide an effective environment not only for those who are climbing up the meritocratic pyramid but also for those who are sliding down it. As personally attained knowledge replaces family inherited capital as a basis for future influence and income, many young persons from affluent families are placed under great pressure to earn for themselves what in earlier times would have been passed on to them. Some will fail in the effort and some will never make the attempt; among these, many will see the causes not in themselves but in the failures of society. The more meritocratic a society becomes — open to talent from all social groups and from men and women alike — and, also, the more static it becomes in creating new positions at the upper levels, the more "sliders" there will be. A few colleges already are largely devoted to a "pay and split" experience for such young persons. How may their "development" best be aided?

4. Purpose 2: Advancing Human Capability in Society at Large

In earlier stages of industrial society, the wealth and potential welfare of a society depended heavily on the amount of physical capital invested and the percentage of the labor force recruited into the modernized sector. The United States now has a high accumulation of capital investment and can add to this accumulation less dramatically year by year. Most of the potential labor force has by now been drawn out of subsistence farming, handicrafts, shopkeeping, and homemaking into rationalized production and service. The new emphasis now needs to be placed, and is being placed, upon enhancing human capability in even more complex ways than through more capital investment and more shifts of people into the commercialized sector, upon intensification of the contributions of individuals, and less on the extensive accumulations of resources. A new stage of development has been entered.

Higher education is involved in this process of advancing human capability through:

Research that provides new ideas and better technology

Service that distributes the new ideas to agriculture, industry, government, the professions, voluntary agencies, and individuals

Finding talent and developing it to its maximum useful level

Aiding talented persons to direct themselves toward the areas of greatest economic and social need

Drawing more people—particularly women and members of underprivileged minority groups—into the active labor force and adding to their geographic and occupational mobility

Adding to the individual skills of persons throughout life and thus to their "social returns" to society, as well as to their individual incomes

Advancing the levels of health of the people through research, training, and advisory service to health care institutions

Providing educational and cultural opportunities for the public at large

Generally adding to the capacity of society to adjust to change, to solve its problems, and to handle emergency situations more effectively

We recognize that there is an overlap between skill training for individual students as part of "educational development," as set forth above, and the provision of high-level manpower for society, but the orientations are different—the one toward meeting the desires of the individual and the other toward satisfying the needs of society.

Higher education was long viewed by many primarily as a method for increasing economic growth, for elevating the gross national product. Attention now needs to move more toward the *net social* product and its enhancement through advancing human capability.

Definition of purpose 2

Higher education has a great responsibility for (1) developing and making available new ideas and new technology, (2) finding and training talent and guiding it to greater usefulness, and (3) generally enhancing the information, the understanding, and the cultural appreciation and opportunities of the public at large.

Performance

In the area of enhancing human capability throughout society, we believe that the performance of higher education, particularly in the century since the land-grant movement, has been at a comparatively superior level among the industrial nations. This is an area, of course, where external support and encouragement make any desirable adjustments to the requirements of society particularly easy and likely within the American context.

The value of university research and service, while clearly substantial, is impossible to calculate with any precision because, among other reasons, its contributions cannot be separated from similar activities of government and industry. However, "advances of knowledge," for which higher education has a significant responsibility, particularly through basic research, have in recent times contributed (along with new capital investment in which the new ideas are embodied) almost one-quarter of the growth of total national income and over one-third of the increase in national income per person employed (Denison, 1967, p. 299). Contributions to productivity in agriculture have been particularly spectacular (Griliches, 1964).

Such contributions require an adequate and steady supply of research funds, particularly from the federal government; an effective distribution of funds on the basis of the ability of the researchers involved rather than on criteria of geographical dispersion; and a constant redistribution of applied research funds to reflect the exhaustion of old ideas and the creation of new ones, and the solution of old problems and the recognition of new ones. We consider to be quite shortsighted recent reductions in the funds available for basic research in the universities. These funds are an excellent investment in the long-run future of the United States and in the welfare of people more generally.

In the United States, service by higher education in the distribution of useful information and advice, historically, has been directed more toward power and toward money than an even-handed policy would warrant. Agriculture and industry and the professions and the federal government have all been able to obtain substantial service, in the form of applied research and consulting advice, from faculty members. Trade unions were for a long time neglected; so were the cities; so, now, are many voluntary agencies and groups. Limitations on service should not be determined, as so often in the past, by the power or wealth of the recipients. Limitations should instead be determined in accordance with the nature of the service to be rendered. It should be limited to advice and to educational efforts, and should not extend into developmental work and actual operations that can be done as well or better by other agencies. But it still takes resources to make service available, and society does not provide the resources on an even-handed basis.

The development of talent is a complex process. First of all those possessing talent must be identified and given a chance to obtain a higher education. Among young people in the top academic talent group (the top one-fifth as identified by standard tests) about 90 percent now attend college; the talent loss within this group is about 10 percent (Wolfle, 1971, p. 105). This is a comparatively good record on an international scale but some loss of talent does occur. Second, in terms of meeting the needs of society for highly trained manpower, only one deficit of substantial importance—in the area of health care—now exists and this deficit will be eliminated by the end of the current decade. Third, more generally, college graduates (particularly women) have a greater propensity to participate in the active labor force, and are more mobile both occupationally and geographically than nongraduates. Fourth, at an overall level, investments in a college education have "social returns" (defined as added economic contributions as against both private and public costs) at a rate somewhere between 13 and 25 percent (Becker, 1964). This is a very substantial rate of return. Added skill, substantially obtained through education, is responsible for about one-sixth of recent increases in total national income, and for about one-fourth of the increases in national income per person employed (Denison, 1967).

Many campuses are now primary cultural centers for their communities, providing resources for the presentation of art, theater, and lectures. With an audience at hand and the capital facilities, many campuses can add substantially to the cultural capability of their communities. Some campuses, however, have neglected this opportunity to enlarge cultural enlightenment and enjoyment. More generally, higher education is a major source of the information and analytical opinion that flows into the public domain. More and more people need more information and more skills more of the time than ever before in order to adjust to, cope with, and perform adequately within the conditions of modern life.

The value of a more educated and better informed human society is incalculable, and we believe that many individuals would be willing to pay a high price for the advantages of living in a society where many, if not most, persons are well-educated, or well-informed, or both. The benefits in terms of mutual tolerance, quality of human services, wide dispersion of cultural facilities, and other forms are substantial. For example, there is both less crime and a lower birthrate among the more highly educated. The general environment for living is enhanced in a well-educated society. Higher education is one of the main ways of keeping a complicated modern society going, through its contributions to preservation of cultural traditions, to development of high skills, to creation of new knowledge.

The gains from higher education in terms of social wealth and welfare are substantial. For a further discussion of performance in this area, see note B in *Technical Notes on Purposes and Performance in Higher Education* (Carnegie Commission on Higher Education, forthcoming).

Recommendation 5: Federal research funds expended within higher education should be maintained steadily at a level of about 0.3 percent of the gross national product.[1]

The Office of Management and Budget, under the general direction of the President, is in the best position to implement this suggested policy.

Recommendation 6: Funds for basic research should be concentrated on highly productive centers and individuals, and money for applied research should be subject to periodic reassignment to reflect the decline of old and the rise of new potentialities.

Recommendation 7: Service should be extended on a more even-handed basis to groups and persons in connection with problems where it may be helpful, subject to the major limitation that any service should be appropriate to the educational functions of higher education.

Recommendation 8: The training of health care personnel should be substantially expanded for the immediate future to eliminate the one remaining major deficit in highly trained manpower.

Recommendation 9: Cultural and "life-long learning" facilities and opportunities should be made available to the general public on an expanded basis.

---

[1] See Carnegie Commission on Higher Education (1970*b*). This is the level of support which prevailed in 1967–68.

5. Purpose 3: Educational Justice for the Postsecondary Age Group

The original element of despotism is a monopoly of talent, which consigns the multitude to comparative ignorance, and secures the balance of knowledge on the side of the rich and the rulers. If then the healthy existence of a free government be, as the committee believe, rooted in the will of the American people, it follows as a necessary consequence, of a government based upon that will, that this monopoly should be broken up, and that the means of equal knowledge (the only security for equal liberty), should be rendered, by legal provision, the common property of all classes . . . until the means of equal instruction shall be equally secured to all, liberty is but an unmeaning word, and equality an empty shadow (Statement by the Workingmen's Labor Party of Philadelphia, 1828).[1]

The United States was the first nation ever formed with the declared intent of assuring social justice to all of its citizens. This historic goal has been raised to new levels of significance in recent years with exploding demands for more equal treatment by the poor, the minorities, and women. What was once a hallowed goal[2] has become a political necessity with a short time horizon for its accomplishment.

Achievement of this goal is essentially a responsibility of society as a whole, not basically a responsibility of education alone. But educational institutions have an obligation to cooperate in this undertaking and even to give leadership to it, both because it is in keeping with their own ideals of human advancement and because

[1] Reproduced in Fine (1961, p. 445).

[2] "When Americans celebrate their national heritage on Independence Day, Memorial Day, or other holidays of this sort they dedicate themselves anew to a nation conceived as the living fulfillment of a political doctrine that enshrines a utopian conception of men's egalitarian and fraternal relations with one another" (Lipset, 1963, p. 75).

it is a legitimate service to society. But society through government must provide the basic policies and the necessary funds.

We delineate educational justice as reasonable equality of opportunity to demonstrate ability, and not as equality of academic results in terms of grades given and degrees awarded to all individuals regardless of performance. Higher education is increasingly important to the realization of social justice so defined. Equality of opportunity means, in particular, equality of opportunity to gain an education and thus to obtain access to better jobs and the potentiality of a more satisfactory life. Majority aspirations of the people were for an elementary education until World War I, for a secondary education until World War II, and now are for postsecondary education. The GI experience after World War II with students coming from families and communities never before in contact with higher education, the Civil Rights movement of the 1950s and 1960s, and now the Women's Liberation movement have all added greatly to the demands for social justice through access to higher education.

Universal access to higher education for high school graduates was assured by the State of California in 1960. Some land-grant universities had opened their doors widely to prospective students much earlier, but places for all students were not guaranteed, and various devices were used to discourage or to deny attendance. Guarantees of places for all high school graduates who wish to attend are now spreading through other jurisdictions—as New York City in 1970—and will continue spreading until they cover the nation. To assure universal access requires both many new places for students and more financial assistance to them. It also requires more attention to the special needs and interests of new groups of students—remedial courses, examination and restructuring of curricula to make certain that the history, culture, and current roles of diverse groups, such as blacks and Chicanos and Indians, are dealt with adequately, among other adaptations.

This Commission has strongly supported universal access to the system of higher education, although it is equally opposed to pressures for universal attendance. It has also strongly supported effective adaptation to the interests of the new students (Carnegie Commission, 1970a). Universal access is likewise strongly supported by faculty members (71 percent), graduate students (88 percent), and undergraduate students (97 percent), according to our Carnegie Commission Survey of Faculty and Student Opinion (see Table 3). Significant numbers of each group—faculty members at the rate of 40 percent, graduate students, 37 percent, and undergraduate students, 29 percent—additionally believe that "more minority group undergraduates should be admitted here even if it means relaxing normal academic standards of admission." Our Commission earlier endorsed such relaxation of admission requirements (ibid.) provided that the prospects were good that the individual student, given appropriate special help, could catch up with his classmates within a reasonable period of time.

Some graduate students (19 percent), some undergraduate students (25 percent), and some faculty members (22 percent) also believe that "normal academic requirements should be relaxed in the appointment of members of minority groups to the faculty here." We believe that more members of minority groups and women should be employed, and that this can be done without lowering the academic standards of the particular institution if these standards are more broadly and more properly defined than they often have been heretofore.

Members of minority groups and women have been subject to adverse discrimination in faculty appointments in the past. We oppose such discrimination. Also, a department or a college can be a better balanced and more effective institution if it draws its faculty from among members of minority groups and from among women as well as from among majority males. Such a department

Table 3 *Faculty and student attitudes on universal access to higher education, on admission of minority group students, and on employment of minority group faculty members*	*Policy*	*Faculty members (percent "yes")*	*Graduate students (percent "yes")*	*Undergraduates (percent "yes")*
	"Opportunities for higher education should be available to all high school graduates who want it."	71	88	97
	"More minority group under-graduates should be admitted here even if it means relaxing normal academic standards of admission."	40	37	29
	"The normal academic requirements should be relaxed in appointing members of minority groups to the faculty."	22	19	25

SOURCE: Carnegie Commission Survey of Faculty and Student Opinion.

or college can, we believe, provide a better environment for all students while also supplying "models" for women students and members of minority groups to try to emulate—but the "models" must be worth emulating academically. Contributions to a better balanced and more effective environment for students should be considered, of course, along with the other more traditional standards of academic performance. These other standards, however, are never fully precise and are always multidimensional, and judgments are often made among people who are reasonably equal in realized and potential talent and performance rather than among a group where each person is "heads-and-shoulders" above each next person with one person being clearly outstanding; there is usually a range of competent and acceptable persons for the particular job within which a choice is made.

We are not suggesting a new basic principle to be made operative in the employment of faculty members. Departments and colleges are always, and quite rightly, concerned with balance—among younger and older faculty members, as between and among fields and points of view and methodologies, as between those who have potential interests in administrative work and those who do not, as between those with special concern for student interests and those without, and in other ways. Balance, and, consequently greater potential effectiveness for the department or college, is a standard criterion in making appointments. The standard question is not whether a candidate is the best single person regardless of field, or age, or interests. The standard question is, rather whether a candidate is the best person for the department or college considering balance and overall effectiveness. We affirm the principle of balance, and we believe it should be extended to consideration also of race and sex where such consideration may add to the effectiveness of the department or college as a whole—where the capacity to inspire students from varied backgrounds is important, and where sensitivity to their special problems and attitudes is needed. We support academic excellence, although we define it somewhat more broadly than has been traditional. The best person should be chosen for the job, but *best* should be defined to include, along with many other characteristics, consideration for the welfare of the entire student group that will be affected.

Thus we believe that members of minority groups and women should be given special consideration in hiring when such persons have the training and the background to perform competently th teaching and research and other assignments of the university or college, and when such special consideration is essential to the creation of a more effective total academic environment. The requirements (1) that members of previously excluded groups be fully competent to perform the tasks for which they are employed and (2) that their employment adds to the effectiveness of the department or college as a whole, obviate the possibility of lowering academic standards by the employment of university and college faculty from among members of groups that were previously excluded or discriminated against.

We are opposed to quotas and to a lottery system. We do not think that all categories of persons necessarily should be equally represented in all activities. People do not all want to do the same things nor are they all equally qualified to do them, but they should have equal chances to satisfy their interests and to qualify for consideration.

We recognize that some members of minority groups and some women (as also some majority males) may have had fewer past opportunities, and may need more assistance (for example, in developing a research record) or more time (for example, a person on a part-time appointment) to show accomplishment than do others. But these are transitional and marginal problems that can be handled within the academic tradition.

Thus we come out in our views about faculty members as we earlier did about students: some special consideration at the point of entry but preservation of the quality of performance. We suggest (1) that a more active search be made than has often been the case in the past for members of minority groups and for women to be placed in the "pool" of candidates for evaluation and (2) that the principle of excellence in the selection of individuals from within this "pool" be retained but that *excellence* be defined more broadly than it usually has been in the past to include consideration of the additional aspects of balance which we have set forth as essential to the most effective overall performance of a department or college.

Once higher education accepts a majority of the postsecondary age group onto its campuses — as it now does in the United States — the situation of the minority remaining outside becomes more serious. Increasingly, members of the noncollege minority may feel deprived in their opportunities and discriminated against because of the subsidies given to the college attenders. Such feelings of deprivation and resentment can only rise to higher and higher levels unless effective action is taken.

Two possible general courses of action are available. One is to move from universal access to universal attendance. This direction of movement we consider highly unwise. Young persons who do not like academic life will become "captives" of it—there are many such reluctant attenders already, and their time and the resources of society will be largely wasted.[3] Too many young people are already victims of the prestige of attending college, and college has been overemphasized as a status-conferring institution. Such students come from families in all socioeconomic groups but perhaps, particularly, from those which are more affluent. Another course of action is to provide more attractive alternative channels of development for young persons—as in apprenticeship programs, service opportunities, and part-time skill training, and with subsidies on the basis of need not unlike those for the college attenders. The logic of the situation points in this direction: concern for the welfare of the entire postsecondary age group as its members try to sort out their opportunities and seek to improve their life chances based on their individual abilities and interests. This is becoming a new imperative. Increasing attention must be paid to the less advantaged as compared with the attention already directed toward the more advantaged.

Higher education—not as a direct purpose but as a consequence of its continued development—affects economic justice more generally. It reduces the scarcity of highly trained manpower and thus, slowly over time and through the imperfect operations of the labor market, diminishes the premiums paid for such skill. It educates people out of reliance on common labor for an income, and thus, by creating a scarcity of people willing to do disagreeable manual work, slowly raises the comparative compensation paid to them. The inevitable consequence is a narrowing of differentials in income orginating from employment. Higher income from the possession of scarce training is comparatively reduced. A democracy lives more peacefully with itself when the distribution of income lies within a reasonably moderate range.

[3] "The growth of enrollments and the movement toward universal higher education has made enrollment in college increasingly obligatory for many students, and their presence there increasingly 'involuntary.' . . . The result is that we are finding in our classrooms large numbers of students who really do not want to be in college, have not entered into willing contract with it, and do not accept the values or legitimacy of the institution" (Trow, 1970).

The impact of higher education on social justice becomes more important all the time. It was less important when land and capital were the main sources of income and influence. Over 90 percent of all gainfully employed persons, however, are now employees and receive most of their income from earnings on their labor; about 70 percent of all income comes from wages and salaries. Thus, equalization of wage and salary differential has become more and more important to the equalization of all income. But the more important consequence of higher education is on the redistribution of incomes among particular individuals, rather than on the relationships among income classes. Higher education is a major means by which individuals seek to locate themselves and do locate themselves among the income classes, some moving up and others moving down; by which they vary their locations from those held by their parents; by which ability and interest rather than inheritance determine location. Thus higher education is more important to equality of individual opportunity in finding a place among the established occupational and income classes, than it is in closing remuneration gaps among these classes—even though it also does this in the long run. Higher education is more concerned with making possible "from each according to his abilities" than in assuring "to each according to his needs."

Higher education is also more important than it once was in the distribution of influence as the "technostructure" has become a more important feature in the application of power in society.

Education is a particularly acceptable way within American democracy of getting greater equality of opportunity among individuals and also one of the more acceptable ways of moving slowly in the direction of more equality of earned income. The changes that take place more nearly affect individuals than they do entire groups and do so over a period of time rather than all at once, correspond more to notions of "fair play," and involve less application of direct control at any moment of time than do most alternative methods.

Higher education is one of the means by which persons, regardless of inherited background, may gain access to the advantages of society, may play a fuller part in society, may be absorbed more congenially within society rather than standing partially rejected outside it.

Higher education is thus called upon, as never before, to be an instrument of justice; to help assure that the disadvantages of the parents shall not necessarily handicap the children; to help assure that merit may have a chance to rise wherever it is found but also that the monetary rewards for it will not be unduly great; to help assure each young person of a reasonable opportunity to develop himself or herself for the sake of his or her quality of life, and for the sake of service to others and to society generally. For higher education to do all this effectively, it must be viewed as one part of a larger system of postsecondary education and, even beyond that, of postsecondary opportunities for all members of the age group. Higher education will increasingly become related to tertiary education and tertiary education to the total opportunity structure for the youth of the nation.

Definition of purpose 3

Higher education has an obligation to join with and to assist other institutions in society in providing educational opportunities for all persons who seek them beyond the secondary level.

Performance

In the area of educational justice, the chance of young persons going to college from families in the lower-half of the income range and from racial and other less advantaged ethnic minority groups (particularly Spanish-speaking) is substantially less than that of young persons from families in the upper-half of the income range and from the historically dominant social group. Inadequate as it is, however, the United States has a better record in providing opportunities for postsecondary education to persons drawn from throughout its population than does any other industrial nation for which data is available.

We believe, first, that concern should be spread from the college-attending group to the total postsecondary age group; second, that adequate provision should be made for several alternative channels into adult life — college being only one, with apprenticeship and service programs being illustrative of other channels; and third, that there should be equal opportunity of access regardless of family income and social background to each of these several channels, including college. Not enough attention is now being accorded to the total postsecondary age group and to the great diversity of interests and talents within it. There has been a clear bias in favor of the academically oriented as traditionally defined and thus of young persons from the more affluent segments of society.

Faculties do not now reflect in their composition, within any reasonable range, the population as a whole. Women have about half the representation that might be expected if no barriers to their talents existed, and members of minority groups have about one-quarter such representation.

Wage and salary differentials in the United States, as in other industrializing nations, have narrowed in the long run as educational opportunities have become more available. Although this narrowing has not continued in the United States during the post-World War II period, when an enormous expansion of occupational openings for college graduates developed, we expect the long-term process to be resumed in the future. This impact on the narrowing of wage and salary differentials should be viewed as an indirect result and not as a direct purpose of higher education.

Higher education, as education more generally, has been a source of greater social justice in the United States, but its task in assisting in the accomplishment of this great national commitment is by no means completed. Higher education, as education generally, can do a great deal to provide equality of opportunity for individuals even in the short run, but it can do only a moderate amount even in the long run to assure greater equality of economic results. The appropriate test to apply to education is its contribution to equality of opportunity for individuals. The test of greater equality of economic results in terms of income is a quite different test and should be applied, to the extent it is to be applied, to a different set of social policies.

For further discussion of performance in this area, see Note C in *Technical Notes on Purposes and Performance in Higher Education* (forthcoming).

Recommendation 10: The total postsecondary age group should become more the subject of concern, and attention should be comparatively less concentrated on those who attend college.

Recommendation 11: Public policy should be directed to improvement of existing channels into adult life and to the creation of new channels—college being only one of several preferred channels.

Recomendation 12: Open-access opportunities should be provided into most and perhaps all of these channels and such access should be subject to public financial support where and as appropriate (Carnegie Commission, 1968, 1970*a*, 1970*b*, 1971*a*, 1971*b*, 1972*b*, 1972*c*), and not restricted to college attendance alone.

Recommendation 13: Admission standards should be relaxed for members of disadvantaged groups, provided that the chances are good that such students can meet graduation requirements in full.

Recommendation 14: Special efforts should be made to find qualified members of minority groups and women for inclusion in the "pool" of candidates for consideration when faculty appointments are being made; and such persons should be given special consideration in employment for faculty positions, where their employment will lead to the creation of a more effective total academic environment for the entire student group that will be affected.

Recommendation 15: Curricula should be examined to be certain they reflect the history, culture, and current roles of minority groups.

We are greatly concerned about equality of opportunity but we are also concerned that the drive for equality of opportunity not take the direction in academic life of destroying standards. The maintenance of standards requires differential treatment in accordance with performance—some students can go further and faster than others. Educational justice does not mean flat equality of results in terms of grades given and degrees earned. People are different in their talents and their interests, and they should be treated differently in proportion to both their talents and their interests. A democracy requires not only equality of opportunity for all its citizens but also special opportunities for what Jefferson called the "aristocracy of talent" provided all persons are given an equal chance to qualify. So also in academic life—special talent should be accorded special opportunities, and it can only be sorted out fairly if standards of performance are maintained. Equality of opportunity and equality of results are not the same thing in academic life—nor anywhere else, and our recommendations are intended to assure the former. Equality of opportunity, given different talents and interests, leads to differentiation in results. Equality of academic results would be, therefore, a denial of equality of opportunity to demonstrate talent and interests.

6. Purpose 4: Pure Learning — Supporting Intellectual and Artistic Creativity

Higher education has become a preeminent location for pure scholarship. This was not always the case. Scientific research began outside the campus, and did not enter the university until the nineteenth century.[1] Much social science and speculative social thought was also accomplished outside the campus—Darwin, Marx, and Freud all worked outside the university. Cultural creativity, also, historically has found its home off campus. All this has changed appreciably and is continuing to change. The campus in the United States has become, and increasingly is, a very productive environment for creativity and reflection in science, social science, the humanities, the creative arts, and social thought. It attracts many of the ablest scholars and many of the more talented artists; it finances them; and it gives them an atmosphere of freedom and encouragement.

As society becomes more dependent upon and devoted to scholarship and creativity, and can better afford to subsidize it, the campus also becomes a more important locus for such activity. "The university is a mechanism for the inheritance of the western style of civilization" (Ashby, 1967), and is the principal means for preserving and extending the "great chain of learning" (Bell, 1971, p. 163). Higher education is now in many countries the preeminent guardian of past, present, and future scholarship. And the United

---

[1] "Up to the middle of the nineteenth century the scientific revolution had left practically untouched the ancient universities of England. The Scottish universities had readily absorbed the new philosophy and faithfully transmitted it, but they did not have the opportunity to become creative centres of scientific thought" (Ashby, 1959, p. 18).

In France, scientific research was concentrated first in the academy, rather than in the universities (Ben-David, 1971, Ch. 6).

States, once culturally dependent on Europe[2] and on the Far East, now is a center in its own right for scholarly and artistic innovation. Once imitative in its culture, the United States has become creative, and the campus is a prime location for this new creativity. The United States now has the wealth and the freedom to encourage curiosity and intellectual explorations wherever talent and sophisticated techniques can carry human thought.

We recognize that pure scholarship in the sense of basic research may later lead to applied research and this in turn to new technology, and that new technology may add to enlarging human capability. But pure scholarship serves its own purpose aside from any subsequent applications it may have, and often arises from different motivations. Thus we list it as a separate purpose, worthy of support, aside from any relations it may have later to applied use.

We recognize also that scholarship and creative artistic activity derive from different traditions, have had quite separate historical relations to academic life, and often are in tension with each other — the scholar in the humanities is often the critic of the creative writer or artist or musical composer, and the creative person often looks down upon such scholarship in the humanities as a dry and pedantic activity. Nevertheless, we have grouped the two together, along with scholarship in basic science and social science. Each of these areas draws upon curiosity and internal inspiration for its motivation. They each required a great deal of freedom from constraints and access to resources that are not dependent upon a demonstrated early "payoff." They each, in their activity, go beyond the other purposes we set forth. Their purpose is more "other worldly" than educating students, or advancing the competency of society, or improving social justice, or criticizing public policy and conduct.

Definition of purpose 4

Higher education has a fundamental obligation to preserve, transmit, and illuminate the wisdom of the past, to find, preserve and analyze the records of the past, to provide an environment for research and intellectual creativity in the present, and to assure for

[2] In the United States, "Not until after the middle of the [nineteenth] century was the German ideal of academic research approved for emulation. . . . Cultural goods can only be imported into friendly markets, and before 1850 our canons of education were not receptive to the idea of academic research" (Hofstadter & Metzger, 1955, p. 376).

the future the trained minds and the continuing interest so that the store of human knowledge may keep on expanding—all this beyond reference to any current practical applications. We include here basic research in science and social science, humanistic scholarship, creative artistic activity, and speculative social thought.

Performance

In the area of pure scholarship, higher education in the United States ranks comparatively well on the world scene—superior in science and the social sciences, more than adequate in the humanities, but only now entering full scale into the creative arts—but even then in advance of higher education in most other nations.

To maintain and improve this record, it is important that funds for basic (as well as applied) research, particularly from federal sources, be available at a reasonable level, that this level be maintained steadily and not be subject to sharp changes which impede the conduct of individual projects and complicate institutional administration, and that funds be distributed increasingly into the areas of the social sciences, humanities, and creative arts. We have noted earlier the very considerable overlap, from an operational point of view, between pure scholarship for "its own sake" and practical research in relation to specific problems.

The continuation of academic freedom is also a prerequisite for creative scholarship. Freedom and money and trained curiosity are the basic resources for scholarship.

For additional comments on performance in the area of scholarship, see Note D in *Technical Notes on Purposes and Performance* (forthcoming).

Recommendation 16: Federal research funds should be substantially increased for the social sciences, humanities, and creative arts from their current level of about 7 percent of the amount for science.

We already have instruments for the expenditure of such funds in the National Science Foundation, the National Endowment for the Humanities, and the National Endowment for the Arts. Support of science should, of course, be continued as we have suggested above.

7. Purpose 5: Evaluation of Society for Self-Renewal— Through Individual Thought and Persuasion

We have chosen the term "evaluation" instead of the more customary one of "criticism" because of the confusion over the so-called critical function of the university. The critical function is (1) sometimes said to be the developing of "critical" minds—the "critical component" as compared with the "technical component" (Keniston & Gerzon, 1971); (2) other times it is said to be the performing of the role of social critic or evaluator by individual faculty members and students; and (3) at still other times it is said to be the undertaking of direct action by the university itself against society—"the critical university." We use the term "evaluation" in the second of these three senses. We include the first as part of educating students. We oppose the third.

The United States has by now largely completed the initial stages of modernization, although this process in never fully completed. But the postmodernized society still has many problems to master: the reduction of poverty, the end of racial, ethnic, and sexual discrimination, the reexamination of values, the renovation of the cities, the conservation of the natural environment, among many others. And, in addition to these specific problems, we face the question of maintaining the flexibility and adaptability in ourselves and in our institutions that will enable us to confront the now unimagined problems and opportunities of the future which rush in at an ever-increasing rate. "Over the centuries the classic question of social reform has been, 'How can we cure this or that specifiable ill?' Now we must ask another kind of question: 'How can we design a system that will continuously reform (i.e., renew) itself, beginning with presently specifiable ills and moving on to ills that we cannot now foresee?'" (Gardner, 1963, p. 5). Any society can atrophy and decline. The capacity of a society to assure its own self-renewal is a critical test of it. Higher education has a part to play in the passing of this test by the United States.

Faculty members have an important role in the processes of national self-renewal. They have, beyond what is available to many others of their fellow citizens, more time, more facilities, more institutional freedom to evaluate specific problems and to suggest remedies, and to assess the society in its totality and to propose improvements. They also have access to something else: "the scientific approach; it does not reject old or accept new hypotheses without publicly tested and logically reproducible evidence; it obliges the enquirer to relate to the specific issue, and not to the person or group from which it emanates; it makes it incumbent on the evaluator to judge on the basis of results, and not on the basis of real or imputed intentions; and it imposes on everyone concerned a humility that comes from knowing that all one's theories have to stand up daily to impartial judgment and may be refuted, and are almost inevitably going to be corrected."[1]

Students share in this effort of self-renewal. They have a chance on campus to develop further their powers of critical appraisal of institutions and their ability to make up their own minds based on facts and analysis. This critical ability, of course, should be held in common by all citizens in a democracy, but college students have a particular current opportunity to refine it.

This purpose of aiding society with the processes of self-renewal, as we view it, does not imply resort to direct political action by institutions of higher education or by their major governmental bodies. We note, however, that about one-third of faculty members now seem to favor the taking of stands on political issues by college and university faculties.[2] Direct institutional political action in our opinion, nevertheless, should be rejected on the basis of any one of six considerations each by itself:

1 That such activity is inconsistent with the free pursuit of new knowledge. It may serve to bind both the institution and its individual members, and thus reduce the truly free pursuit of truth by the latter. Learning may be impaired.

[1] Written comment by Joseph Ben-David, University of Chicago, October 23, 1972.

[2] To the statement that "It is desirable for college and university faculty to put themselves on record by vote in major political controversies," 32.7 percent of faculty members stated agreement. (Lipset & Ladd, 1972). Institutions of higher education do, of course, have an obligation to take positions on matters which affect them as institutions, such as their budgets, their independence, and their purposes.

2 That such activity could tear institutions of higher education apart internally as they sought to take positions. Effective governance may be impaired.

3 That such activity would often be counterproductive in achieving its immediate aims because society would not follow along and might even do just the opposite—academic rhetoric is less effective than academic scholarship. Even if it is specifically productive, such activity would be more generally counterproductive because it would likely lead to less support for and more external controls over higher education, and to a general estrangement of higher education from society. Institutional ventures into political influence violate the principle of institutional neutrality which is essential to the political separation from the state. Independence may be impaired.

4 That political positions taken by academic bodies are likely to be issued at a moment of intense crisis and in a setting where there is no direct responsibility for effectuating the position, and thus are not fully likely to be the result either of scholarly reflection or of operational accountability. They may thus not be representative of the best efforts of the scholarly world and yet they may be given visibility as though they were. Higher education should reflect on such episodes as the endorsement by the faculty of the University of Paris of the finding of Joan of Arc as guilty of heresy and witchcraft, and of faculty support for Hitler in Germany (Machlup, 1971, pp. 18 and 24). Higher education has fought long and hard to free itself from the parochialism of time and place; to free itself from church and state in the name of independent scholarship. The exercise of judgment may be impaired.

5 That the purpose of government is to make good use of the application of power, but that the purpose of higher education is to make good use of the search for truth. These are two quite different and even inconsistent activities. Just as it is unwise for government to interfere directly in the search for truth within higher education, it may be equally unwise for institutions of higher education to try to interfere directly in the application of power by government. If the two are to be mixed, the chance that political power may corrupt the search for truth is greater, however, than that academics may control power. And the exercise of power often leads to entanglements in hypocrisy. The sense of integrity may be impaired.

6 There are other, and better ways, in which academic persons, in their roles as citizens, can pursue political influence, as through political parties and other action groups.

The methods, consequently, that should be chosen are those of careful thought, empirical evidence, logical argument, and persuasion by individuals and by voluntary groups. These are the methods, also, of pure scholarship. As we view it, individual acts of evaluation should grow primarily out of pure scholarship as the source of their inspiration. We thus support a "constructive dissent which fulfills one overriding condition: it must shift the state of opinion about the subject in such a way that other experts in the subject are prepared to concur. This is done either by producing acceptable new data or by reinterpreting old data in a convincing way. It is a very austere form of dissent and it is difficult to learn. But it is this discipline of dissent which has rescued knowledge in fields as wide apart as theology and physics, from remaining authoritarian and static" (Ashby, 1969, p. 64).

Academic persons, *qua* academic persons, should pursue truth not power. "To politicise the universities would be to destroy their prime social purpose" (ibid., p. 65). Only in the nonpoliticized university can scholars "reflect without having to decide, observe without having to participate, criticize without having to reform"; only in such a university can they be fully able to "reflect and observe without prejudice and to criticize without fear"; and these qualities of academic life should be cherished, "for without disinterested and fearless criticism society will lose its power of self renewal" (Ashby, 1967, p. 116).

Effective evaluation of society is more likely to originate in high quality scholarship than in a potentially self-destructive pursuit of political commitment by academic institutions. " . . . the price which a university pays for acquiring power outside its walls is loss of freedom. If the university, as a corporate body, puts its weight behind any pressure group or any political party . . . it compromises its freedom" (Ashby & Anderson, 1970, p. 150).

We note that faculty members generally (61 percent) and also undergraduate students (66 percent) believe that "this institution should be actively engaged in solving social problems" (Carnegie Commission Survey of Faculty and Student Opinion). We agree with this within the limitations we have already set forth of avoidance of institutional commitment to specific points of view, of foundation on scholarship, of reliance on persuasion.

We also note, however, that significant numbers of faculty members responded in the Carnegie Commission Survey of Faculty and Student Opinion, to questions which carry implications about their degree of acceptance of democratic processes of change as follows (see Table 4 for comparison with responses of undergraduate and graduate students):

Percent who *disagreed* with the statement that "In the U.S.A. today there can be no justification for using violence to achieve political goals."	27 percent
Percent who *agreed* with the statement that "Faculty members should be free on campus to advocate violent resistance to public authority."	22 percent
Percent who *disagreed* with the statement that "Students who disrupt the functioning of a college should be expelled or suspended."	20 percent
Percent who *agreed* with the statement that "Meaningful social change cannot be achieved through traditional American politics."	33 percent

Taken together these responses imply that a sizable number of faculty members have impaired confidence in American democratic processes, and may share some sympathy for action outside the limits we have set forth for peaceful persuasion through individual efforts. We recognize that no single one of these questions is properly phrased to indicate precisely a rejection of a scholarly approach to evaluation of society, but the replies to these questions, taken together with the replies relating to the question of going on record on political controversies, do imply that one-fifth to one-third of faculty members may have a more activist view of the "critical function" of higher education than is contained within the scholarly approach to the function as we understand it. The distribution of faculty on a "radicalism scale" varies substantially from one classification to another, and, thus, overall figures are not reflective of the great internal variations that exist (see Table 5).

These figures require several caveats if any one were to seek to predict future behavior from them:

They result from questionnaires circulated in the period 1969 to 1972, which was a very special period in American history.

People change their opinions over time.

Times change.

People do not always act in fact in the way they indicate by their respo:
to questions.

There may be no future periods which will test actions versus questi
naire responses.

If such future periods do occur, the students at such times might damp
rather than stimulate, faculty political activism; unionization, if it spre:
widely, may become a restraining force, as in other segments of Ameri
society; and the labor market may make the costs of political activi
greater than in the 1960s.

What may look like a generally consistent point of view in the abse:
of an actual situation that stimulates action, may turn out to be a conge:
of different points of view when the prospect of action becomes a real
there may be great factional controversy about means and ends and timi

TABLE 4 Academic attitudes on use and advocacy of violence, on disruption of campus, and on source of social change	Position	Faculty members	Graduate students	Undergrad: students
	"In the U.S.A. today there can be no justification for using violence to achieve political goals." (Percentage responding "disagree")	27	*	25
	"Faculty members should be free on campus to advocate violent resistance to public authority." (Percentage responding "agree")	22	23	32
	"Students who disrupt the functioning of a college should be expelled or suspended." (Percentage responding "disagree")	20	27	39
	"Meaningful social change cannot be achieved through traditional American politics." (Percentage responding "agree")	33	38	55

* Question not asked.
SOURCE: Carnegie Commission Survey of Faculty and Student Opinion.

	Percent of faculty members in
TABLE 5 *Distribution of faculty on "radicalism scale"—selected classifications* Classification	scales 1 and 2

Classification	Percent of faculty members in scales 1 and 2
Age	
60 and over	6
Under 30	17
Field	
Social sciences	20
Humanities	17
Fine arts	14
Education	10
Physical sciences	9
Biological sciences	8
Medicine	6
Law	6
Business	5
Agriculture	3
Social psychology	39
Social work	30
Sociology	25
Political science	24
Philosophy	24
Art	18
History	17
Economics	15
Music	9
Chemistry	8
Civil engineering	5
Physical education	4
Botany	3
Home economics	2

SOURCE: Carnegie Commission Survey of Faculty and Student Opinion. "Radicalism Scale"—with scale 1 (highest) to 5 (lowest) constructed by Ladd-Lipset from answers to four statements and questions: "In the U.S.A. today there can be no justification for using violence to achieve political goals"; "Meaningful social change cannot be achieved through traditional American politics"; "Most American colleges and universities are racist whether they mean it or not"; and "What do you think of the emergence of radical student activism in recent years?" These four questions are *not* the same set of questions as in Table 4 and in the text, but the general ranking of classifications would almost certainly be substantially the same if they were.

What these figures do say is that there has recently been a di
sensus within the American professoriate over attitudes towar
society and toward professorial conduct in relation to society an
to the campus. Almost certainly this dissensus has been great
than ever before in history. Thus the performance of the evaluati
purpose may now take place within a different and more difficu
context of faculty attitudes than in earlier times.

Members of the academic community should keep in mind (
that they are not the only people in society with a right to evalua
society—this is a general obligation of all citizens—and (2) tha
they have not necessarily been endowed either with a higher sens
of morality or the quality of better generalized judgment than oth
persons in society. They have no special monopoly on either m
rality or judgment, and it can be self-defeating to cherish and
assert any such illusions. Members of the academic communi
are different only in the time, the facilities, and the institution
freedom at their disposal. The availability of each of these asse
increases the need for their effective and responsible use.

With all these qualifications in mind, however, higher educatic
does have as one of its purposes the defense of the right of an
provision of facilities for evaluation of society, in its componer
parts and in its totality, by its faculty members and its studen
in their individual capacities.

Definition of purpose 5

Faculty members and students, as an integral part of their scho
arly activities, should have both the freedom and the opportuni
to engage in the evaluation of society through individual thoug
and persuasion.

Performance

In the area of the critical evaluation of society, we see two maj
problems: one is that the public does not fully understand or acce
this purpose of higher education and the other is that some el
ments on some campuses exploit the opportunity unwisely and eve
illegally.

The answers to the first problem are more public discussion
the constructive possibilities and even urgent necessities inhere
in this form of service—it does, however, come as a shock to mar
people when academics use their knowledge to criticize socie

rather than alone to support it in what it wants to do—and firm protections for the academic freedom of faculty members and for the essential independence of the campus.

The second problem requires better rules and more self-restraint on campus. Critical evaluation should not be allowed to extend to disruption of the campus or of society, to the improper use of campus facilities to mount public campaigns for or against some idea or program or political candidate, to the indoctrination of students to some one point of view on threat of lower academic rewards, to use of political tests for preferment among faculty members, or to the commitment of the institution as such to any single program of social change. The role of the campus is to encourage the offering of facts and ideas, not to seek to compel the acceptance of facts and ideas by society. Members of the academic community should rely on wisdom and persuasion, not slogans and power. The course of pursuing power is not only out of keeping with the nature of the campus as an academic institution, but is self-defeating, both internally and externally.

The critical evaluation of society has been in good supply in recent years, even though often less constructive and effective than might ideally be desired. The campuses have in recent times, however, been centers for the critical evaluation of American society in such areas of great central concern as civil rights, war and peace, and conservation of the environment.

Recommendation 17. The principles of academic freedom for faculty members should be preserved where they are now effective and extended into areas where they do not now prevail, and the essential institutional independence of the campus should be fully protected by society to assure the continuance of the possibilities of critical evaluation of society by individual faculty members and students.[3]

Recommendation 18: Each institution of higher education should establish a policy of self-restraint against disruptive activities, against improper use of campus facilities, against improper political indoctrination of students, against selection and promotion of faculty members in accordance with their political beliefs, and

[3] See the suggestions in Carnegie Commission (1973).

against commitment of the institution as such to the pursuit specific external political and social changes; each institution should be prepared to defend its own integrity.[4]

This is a particular responsibility of faculty members, who should be prepared to recognize the important distinctions (a between corporate action and individual action and (b) between acting as a scholar and acting as a citizen.[5]

The conduct of this purpose will always arouse tensions on campus and in society—it provides an eternal battleground for contending points of view; and it requires the drawing of fine distinctions. Broadly speaking, however, there are three basic positions that can be taken: the first is that neither the institution nor its members should criticize society—this cannot be enforced in democracy; the second is that both the institution and its members can and should engage in the criticism of society—and even action against it—either occasionally or even constantly; and the third is that individual members, but not the institution or its corporate bodies, can and even should engage in critical activity. We support the last of these positions, subject to the application of reasonable rules. But this is inherently a difficult purpose to carry out; there is already disagreement in the United States today over specific rules and distinctions, and, in addition, a substantial minority of faculty members appears to be in dissensus with the majority of faculty members over the basic position to be taken.

[4] See the suggestions in Carnegie Commission (1971c & 1972a).

[5] For a discussion of the differences between acting as a "citizen" and acting as a "member of a learned profession" see Van Alstyne (1972).

8. Purposes:
Approaching the Year 2000

The possibilities of contributions by higher learning to the needs of society change both as higher learning accumulates more knowledge and new methodologies, and as society evolves and becomes a more intricate web of activities and relationships. Thus the purposes of higher education as seen from different cultural perspectives and as accumulated over the centuries should be reevaluated periodically. Such a review is now going on in any event on campus and in society. Students and faculty members have aspirations which are not now being fully met, as we have noted above. The public has become generally more questioning than it was in earlier times about the purposes of higher education, and about some of the negative results as seen from its point of view. Also, society is changing in many ways, including more education per capita, more affluence, more urbanization, constantly newer technology (particularly in the electronic field), higher aspirations among women and minority group members, a new labor market situation for college graduates, new styles of life, a new consciousness about the environment, a new interest in designing the future through the hand of man, among many others. In total, these forces will change the surrounding society substantially and thus will have indirect as well as direct impacts on the purposes of higher education.

The major purposes of higher education for the rest of this century, as we have set them forth in the preceding sections, are complex. This has been the case in the United States for a long time. In few countries has higher education taken on, largely of its own accord, such major responsibilities for service to society and for equality of opportunity as it has in the United States.

It is much easier to evaluate a system that has simpler responsibilities—a system, for example, that has the duty to supply high-level manpower and to teach a set ideological doctrine, as in Russia;

or a system, as another example, that prepares students largely fc teaching positions and the civil service, and instructs them in th history and content of a single high culture, as historically i France. The assignments are specific and the tests of accomplish ment are relatively precise.

The American situation is quite different—assignments are mor self-imposed, or at least more subject to voluntary acceptance, an comparatively quite complex, and the tests of performance, as consequence, quite varied. And, as compared with other types c social institutions, such as the corporation or the political party there is no comparatively simple test of profits accrued or vote won.

The purposes of higher education in the United States are plura the constituent institutions are diverse, and performance is sub ject to many interpretations. We have provided above our own ir terpretation of performance as related to each of the major purpose of higher education as we see them. The overall performance c higher education in the United States, as we evaluate it: (1) has bee superior in the areas of pure scholarship and of advancing huma capability throughout society; (2) has been generally satisfactor in the area of the educational advancement of students but wit major improvements possible; (3) has been least adequate in th area of educational justice—although major improvements are nov underway; (4) has been most uncertain in the area of providing ar effective environment for the developmental growth of students – where so little of certainty is known; and (5) has been most uneven most controversial, and most in need of clarification in the are of assistance in the critical evaluation of society. We are convince that performance, whatever its current level, can be improved in each of these areas of high purpose. Higher education in the Unite States, particularly since 1870, has demonstrated a moderate ca pacity for responding to pressures for reform beginning with th land-grant movement, more recently with the move toward univer sal access, and through many other changes in between. Whil many of the changes which have taken place have been accom plished under external encouragement and pressure, higher educa tion has not been as rigid as in some other nations where only . social cataclysm has disrupted the historical tenor of its ways—fo example, the Napoleonic revolution in France or the Leninis revolution in Russia. American higher education fortunately ha been subject and is now subject to continuing internal reform, albeit at times quite slow and quite modest.

On the continuum that goes from the faithful reproduction of society as it exists to the attempted production of a totally new form of society, higher education in the United States has stood more or less midway. It has been engaged in supporting society as well as in changing it. It has sought to perfect the traditional status quo—particularly before 1870 with its emphasis upon the higher culture and the moral person—but it has also altered the traditional status quo through the impacts of research and increased access to knowledge—particularly since 1870.

We expect that, in the future, higher education will demonstrate an equal or perhaps even greater willingness to accept the need for continuing reform and an equal or perhaps even greater capacity to help shape the society of the future—even more than it has since 1870. In this conviction, we have, earlier in this report, made a series of recommendations—recommendations designed to improve the performance of each of the purposes.

Part Two:
Functions

9. The Historical Process of Accumulating Purposes in the American Context

Higher education in North America began with the founding of Harvard in 1636. The college pattern was basically taken from Stuart England with some Scottish influence. The curriculum was largely concerned with the Bible, with European and classical culture, with Greek and Latin, and with mathematics. The purpose was to maintain the old culture brought from England into the middle of a wilderness. "We in this country," wrote Jonathan Mitchell, "being far removed from the more cultivated parts of the world, had need to use utmost care and diligence to keep up learning and help to education among us, lest degeneracy, barbarism, ignorance and irreligion do by degrees break in upon us."[1] A broad general education was combined with a deep concern for the moral and religious development of youth, and out of this concern grew the many rules that stood *in loco parentis.* Thus an original purpose of American higher education was *personal development* through acculturation to the classics and to moral principles.[2]

This purpose of personal development has continued ever since in changing forms. Acculturation came to mean less an indoctrination into the classics and more a general grasp of the newer subjects of science and social science, as well as the older humanities, and of the precepts of American democracy and society as it evolved. Acculturation in any specific nationalistic sense gradually became less important as America became more pluralistic in its patterns, and, to some extent, in recent times, also less sure of itself.

[1] See Jonathan Mitchell, "A Modell for the Maintaining of Students & Fellows of Choise Abilities at the Colledge in Cambridge," probably in 1663, *Publications of the Colonial Society of Massachusetts,* XXXI (1935), p. 311; quoted in Cremin (1970, pp. 176–177).

[2] See Handlin and Handlin (1970) for a history of acculturation as a function of American colleges.

The definition of personal development has changed in other ways. *In loco parentis* rules were gradually relaxed, as students took over more control of their own collegiate lives. After a period between the Civil War and World War I, during which, following the model of the German university, the larger American institutions tended to treat students as independent adults, there came a movement to reintegrate the campus and the classroom, and advising and counseling services—the "student personnel movement"—took the place of the older and more rigid custodial roles of the colleges.[3] The "independence" phase of student life was accompanied by a great rise in extracurricular activities, reaching a peak in the 1920s and giving a new dimension to development in athletics, journalism, theater, student government, and other areas.

As new students have come in, some of them uncommitted to an academic or professional life, and as all students face more life choices, the campus has become more of a place for the search for identity—an interlude between family influence and adult commitment to an occupation and to a way of life. It has become more of a way station where young people can assay the alternatives before them in their greater and greater variety. Also, personal development, for some, now means a chance to make up for past skill deficiencies through remedial work. Thus, personal development has been a continuing but changing theme of higher education in the United States.

A second theme was also introduced early, and this was the *economic* one. Benjamin Franklin spoke of education as the "best investment." Concerned with education for practical pursuits— crafts, vocations, industries—he thought that through education, available to all in accord with their individual talents, would come a free and wealthy society. But like so many other features of modern American higher education, the economic purpose was principally developed in the late nineteenth century: after the joining of the ancient strands of science and technology, after the invention

---

[3] "When the personnel movement arose in the twentieth century, it thus represented not only a major effort to restore unified life to the American college but also a revival of the old-time college's concern for the non-intellectual side of the student's career. This reaction to the temporary vogue of German impersonalism expressed itself, however, in different ways from the clerically dominated pattern of earlier times" (Brubacher & Rudy, 1968, p. 331).

of how to invent,[4] and after more and more occupations began to draw on the theoretical base which universities could supply and thus began to become professions. The early college students had been headed for the historic professions of teaching, preaching, law, and medicine; after the Civil War, with the land-grant movement and the industrialization of the United States, selecting and training the ablest students for the many new occupations, and conducting research for the sake of national wealth and welfare also became acknowledged functions of the university. This economic purpose increased its momentum during and after World War II, with the emphases upon research and development, and upon preparing highly trained "manpower." The economic purpose became, for a time, the most favored purpose of all.

A third theme was especially favored by Jefferson. He saw education as fulfilling a *political role.* The role was threefold: to give all citizens an education so that they could be effective participants in a democracy—"liberty can never be safe but in the hands of the people themselves, and that too of the people with a certain degree of instruction";[5] to find and to train the "natural aristocracy" of talent for positions of leadership, and to assure some equality of opportunity so that deprivations in one generation need not necessarily be passed on to members of succeeding generations. Higher education has had an increased part to play, particularly in the third of these political roles—providing greater equality of opportunity—as the United States began moving after World War I from elite to mass higher education and then, after World War II, from mass to universal-access higher education.

A further political purpose has been introduced more recently—the evaluative or critical function. As faculty members in the late nineteenth century began to see themselves more as trained professionals and less as employees of religious denominations or private interests, and as interest in the social sciences grew, faculty members began evaluating the surrounding society generally and specifically. Critical remarks made in and out of the classroom, however, often led to confrontation with the university's business supporters, and sometimes to the professor's dismissal. A landmark

---

[4] "The greatest invention of the nineteenth century was the invention of the method of invention" (Whitehead, 1939, p. 141).

[5] Letter to George Washington, January 4, 1786, in Boyd, ed. (1950, vol. 9, p. 151).

episode was the forced resignation of Professor Edward A. Ross by Stanford University for his "rabid" ideas.[6] This and other cases led to greatly increased efforts to protect academic freedom.

As academic freedom became better protected, particularly through the efforts of the American Association of University Professors and the decisions of the courts, and as the formation of national policies has come to rely more on expert advice, the evaluative purpose of higher education has been more greatly emphasized. The other purposes arose largely out of the concerns of society, but this purpose was largely generated internally. Yet it is a national purpose. Society needs self-renewal, and academic evaluation and criticism constitute one source of self-renewal. As some other sources of independent appraisal have become less active, such as the unions and the press, individuals on the campus have become more of a needed source of social commentary.

A fourth purpose was added with the national endorsement of the land-grant movement, and this was *service to the surrounding society.* It began with service to agriculture, moved on to industry and the professions, came to encompass the federal government particularly during the New Deal and World War II, and the service function now is reaching into the cities and environmental protection. Along the way, the campus also became a cultural and entertainment center for the surrounding community through its theaters, its lectures, its athletic games, and in other ways.

The logic of this service orientation was clear. More problems required more research for their solution and the campus was the chosen—but not exclusive—national instrument for basic research (Wolfle, 1972). Also, the campus had ready-made audiences for cultural and entertainment events, and could readily accept members of the public at them as well as members of the campus.

Accumulating purposes

One purpose has been added to another—personal development, economic growth, political health, service to society—and each pur

[6] "At a time when the conservative community thought Eugene V. Debs the incarnate devil, Ross publicly defended him; in a university that had been founded by a railroad Republican whose ventures had depended on free labor, he advocated municipal ownership of utilities and a ban on Oriental immigration. At a time when most economists were for McKinley and gold, he wrote a tract in favor of free silver that was used by the Democratic party" (Hofstadter & Metzger, 1955, p. 438).

pose has become more complex: thus the historical process of proliferating purposes.

Fifty percent of youth now enter college instead of the two percent or less of a century ago, personal development is a more complex process with fewer accepted rules for conduct, and there are more occupational alternatives from which to choose.

Economic advancement of the nation is now more tied to greater skill and better technology, and less to quantitative additions of labor and capital alone (and thus is more tied to training and research in higher education), as compared with the period before the Great Depression.

The demand for equality of opportunity is more insistent and higher education is more of a door to opportunity, particularly since World War II.

The nature of society is more in question and constructive evaluation more necessary to its self-renewal, particularly since the 1960s.

Problems are more complicated, and new skills and new ideas are more essential to their amelioration; and this will come to be more and more the case.

Higher education can now do more for more people and for more parts of society and for society as a whole in these several ways than ever before. Its purposes have, as a consequence, grown in complexity. Some regret this, others welcome it. But, either way, it is an overwhelming fact of life for higher education and for American society. Higher education was once on the periphery of the life of the middle classes; it is now more at the center of the entire society. The more that society needs new knowledge and high skills, the more central it becomes. Purposes accumulate as the trained intellect becomes more essential to the effective conduct of society.

The four historical purposes that have accumulated may be partially translated into the five current and future purposes which we earlier set forth as follows:

- Personal development can be translated into the education of the individual student and the provision of an environment for developmental growth
- Economic advancement, into aspects of advancing human capability in society at large

- Political health, in part, into educational justice and into evaluation of society
- Service to society, into aspects of advancing human capability

Pure scholarship has come along more as a companion of these four historical purposes than as a consciously chosen purpose by American society. We believe, however, that it should now be set forth formally as a central purpose, as we have done above.

10. *Functions Actually Performed Within the System of Higher Education*

Related to the purposes set forth in the previous section is a whole series of functions directly related to carrying them out. These direct functions are supplemented by support functions such as business services, library services, public relations services, and "custodial" services like feeding and housing. Ancillary functions, such as operation of a governmental laboratory, are also sometimes carried out. We shall be concerned here only with the direct functions. We set forth below the major ones now performed within higher education to indicate their complexity, and as background for consideration of certain of these functions and of problems related to their combination with each other.

Education of students and provision of a constructive environment for developmental growth:

1   General education or what we have called "broad learning experiences"—the provision of opportunities to survey the cultural heritage of mankind, to understand man and society

2   Specialized academic and occupational preparation—the offering of programs in depth that advance specialized academic and occupational interests

3   Academic socialization—the establishment and application of a set of rules and standards which govern academic conduct

4   Campus environment—provision of a series of activities, such as cultural, athletic, work, and service opportunities, and a set of personal relationships which provide an interesting and stimulating environment

5   Personal support—making available informal and formal advisory and counseling services.

6 "Holding operation" or period of "moratorium"—providing for students a period to assess options and make choices before committing themselves to occupations, styles of life, and marriage partners; a period for maturation

Advancing human capability in society at large:

7 Research—particularly research that adds directly or indirectly to human health, welfare and wealth

8 Service—advice and instruction to persons and organizations external to the campus

9 Sorting talent—finding talent, guiding and rating it, and placing it in productive occupations

10 Training in vocational, technical, preprofessional, and professional skills

11 Cultural advancement—provision of cultural and informational facilities and personnel

Assistance with the provision of educational justice:

12 Development of an adequate number of places—particularly of the open-access type

13 Development of appropriate special programs—both remedial and cultural

14 Financial support—making available funds to cover essential costs of students

Providing an effective locus for pure scholarship and artistic creativity:

15 Provision of facilities and personnel and a favorable climate for the advancement of pure scholarship, in the sense of scholarship that is motivated by a desire to enhance the cultural heritage and respond to human curiosity and add to wisdom, and of artistic creativity

Providing an effective locus for evaluation of society:

16 Provision of freedom, of opportunities, and of reasonable rules of conduct relating to such evaluation

These several functions relate back to purposes and ahead to such issues as governance and finance. Some functions, such as development of open-access places and conduct of research projects, by their very nature, tend to draw governmental control or influence; others, such as pure scholarship and professional training, inherently, lead to strong faculty influence and control; and still others, such as development of special remedial and ethnic-study programs, attract student attention. This all leads to different governance patterns in different types of endeavors, for example: to faculty domination of All Souls College at Oxford, to strong governmental influence over a large research laboratory, which it fully supports, to student participation in a black studies program. Governance following functions also leads to broad general shifts: to more governmental influence when the research function is greatly increased and when educational justice becomes a much greater public concern; to more student participation as the "developmental growth" of students engages more campus attention; to less influence for the office of the traditional dean of students as *in loco parentis* rules have faded away but more influence to the new "student affairs officers" in their efforts to advise and assist students. As functions go, to some extent, so too does governance.

The same is also true of financing. The expansion of research and of provisions for educational justice draws more federal money. Pure scholarship relies more on endowments and foundation support. Enrichment of the campus environment and enlargement of personal support activities usually requires funds from student tuitions and alumni gifts. Financing also, in part, follows functions. As functions change, the sources of money follows these changes.

Public opinion is affected, for example, as the evaluative function becomes a more active one. Student attitudes are changed where research draws attention away from the education of the undergraduate. The community college segment expands as educational justice is more greatly emphasized. Health science centers expand as advancing human capability through better health is viewed as more important. Policies are affected as, among many other possible illustrations, attention to educational justice brings in a more varied student body; and as attention to the developmental growth of students puts a high premium on more varied options for students.

The long arm of changing purposes reaches into changing functions, and changing functions, in turn, reach into many aspects of the higher education endeavor. Purposes are basic to nearly all else.

11. *Functions—Contradictions, Comparative Effectiveness, and Complementary Combinations*

Any institution—not just an institution of higher education—may take on more functions than it can effectively accommodate. Much of industry at one time operated paternalistic "company towns" where the employer was also landlord, merchant, and police chief. This proved to be unwise from many points of view and has been universally abandoned in the United States. Institutions of higher education now also face the question of whether they, too, should abandon some of their accumulated functions.

The growth of functions, often unplanned,[1] has resulted from several forces: (1) a function once taken on is seldom later dropped by higher education, although old-style *in loco parentis* responsibilities have been largely eliminated—there is no self-destruct mechanism, no moral equivalent of bankruptcy; (2) higher education has done many things very well; (3) society, as a consequence, has developed great faith in higher education and has assigned to it many functions on the basis of this faith, such as the operation of defense-related laboratories—thus the "halo effect"; (4) some functions have been added as the result of default by other institutions—such as remedial work; and (5) some functions have been taken on out of the sheer instinct for aggrandizement—like unnecessary Ph.D. programs.

The accumulation of functions by an institution adds to its complexity, to greater size and thus to more levels of bureaucracy, to divided attention by top administrators, and to uncertain loyalties. It may also lead to contradictions in purposes, to inefficiencies in operation, and to inconsistencies among activities. We believe the rule should be: only necessary and compatible functions—they have

---

[1] Eric Ashby speaks of this as the "accretion of functions over the centuries" beginning with Salerno and Bologna (Ashby, 1959, p. 68).

proved hard enough to handle. Higher education generally and each campus specifically should not overextend itself.

From the point of view of society, even an industrially advanced nation could conceivably get along without any system of higher education or at least without a highly developed one. The sorting out of students and their acculturation to society could take place largely at the secondary and primary levels, as in Japan. Vocational and occupational training could take place within industry and governmental ministries, and professional training within the professions on an apprenticeship basis. Research could be handled by government agencies or by industry or by scientific academies — or research results could be imported from abroad. Service activities could be provided by consulting firms and government agencies. Critical evaluation could come from sources other than higher education. A substantial disaggregation of the functions of higher education, from the viewpoint of a society, is possible in theory.

In practice, some nations, such as Japan and Germany, have made enormous advances since World War II in economic growth and even in democratic development without having really absolutely first-rate systems of higher education. Other nations, such as Britain, with first-rate systems have at the same time made lesser comparative progress. One large nation, China, virtually dismantled its system of higher education and has now only partially restored it without any disastrous short-term consequences. Another large nation, Russia, has only a very partial system of higher education by American standards—only the professional training and attempted political indoctrination of high-level manpower. Higher education is one way of providing for the performance of certain functions but not the only way.

While a massive disaggregation of the functions performed by higher education in the United States is theoretically possible, we believe it would be highly unwise. The campus is the best single place for the conduct of pure scholarship; higher education is essential to advancing social justice; research and service and technical training have been conducted at high levels of competence; and the self-renewal of the nation benefits from the critical evaluations originating on campus. But the United States, as other nations, could survive with a less complex—possibly even much less complex—system of higher education than it now has.

We do not suggest an approach of substantial disaggregation but we do suggest that all functions now being performed should not necessarily be taken for granted; that each function should be subject to periodic scrutiny by each institution of higher education.

Contradictions and comparative effectiveness in the performance of the functions of higher education

The campus is primarily an academic institution. We consider it a contradiction when the campus takes on functions which are at odds with the inherent nature of academic life. We also consider it inefficient when an academic institution takes on nonacademic operations which can be performed as well or better by other institutions.

We place in the first category all secret research, for secrecy is abhorrent to the search for truth when results must be open to analysis and comment to test whether they be the truth or not.

We place in the second category operational activities, such as administering governmental developmental laboratories, and the running of food services and operation of housing facilities, if and when there is no directly academic activity involved.

We propose two tests: (1) Is the activity, even if largely academic in method or content, compatible with the mores of academic life? and (2) Is the activity, if not academic in method or content, better done by the campus than by any other alternate agency? If the answer is "no" in specific cases to either question, we believe there is a prima facie case for disengagement.

Some campuses have become much more involved in activities potentially peripheral to strictly academic functions than have others. This is particularly true of the large research universities (secret research and the operation of production-oriented laboratories) and the small residential liberal arts colleges (the operation of living and eating facilities). The impact of these involvements, because of their scale, is far greater, however, on the big research universities; the problem of institutional overloading is concentrated there in particular.

Disaggregation of functions is not an easy task. Sometimes excess functions can be turned over to existing governmental or commercial or cooperative agencies. Other times it will be more feasible to create quasi-university agencies—like quasi-public corporations —to operate them, where the campus has a continuing elemental responsibility but no direct operational involvement. Often, however, the lack of an alternative agency or a long history of involvement or intricate interrelationships will make disengagement very

difficult and even impossible. Since disengagement can be so difficult, new engagements deserve the most careful scrutiny.

Recommendation 19: Each institution of higher education should
survey periodically the totality of the functions it performs to be
sure that none of them contradict the ethos of academic life, and
that none of the nonacademic functions could be as well or better
performed by some quasi-university or external agency.

Recommendation 20: All secret research should be eliminated from
all campuses as a matter of national policy, except under quite
unusual circumstances.

Recommendation 21: Campuses should not add and, where feasible, should eliminate, operational, custodial, and service functions
which are not directly tied to academic and educational activities
and which can be performed as well or better by other agencies.

**Complementary combinations of the functions performed on a single
campus**

Certain functions may be appropriate for the totality of higher
education but may not fit well together on a single campus. For
example, the faculty mentality that goes along with highly specialized research institutes is often inconsistent with that of a liberal
arts college devoted to the education of generalists; careful attention
to remedial work is not likely to be forthcoming from a faculty
engaged in pure scholarship; and vocational training calls for quite
different faculty skills and interests than does Ph.D. training. The
faculty members and the students drawn to these contrasting
activities have such different interests that they are not likely to mix
well with each other, to develop a sincere concern for each other's
welfare, or to make jointly effective policy concerning the disparate
functions. Gross inconsistencies should be avoided as divisive
within the institution and as counterproductive for all concerned.

Differentiation of functions among institutions helps to provide
diversity among them and to reduce the tendency toward homo-
genization.

The search for excellence can be aided by specialization which
allows not only concentration of attention and effort, but also a
higher status for some endeavors than they would have if they
were subordinated to others in the same institution. Technical

training, for example, may need its own protected enclave if it is not to be subordinated to more academic pursuits. Pure research, as another example, with its elitist connotations, may need protection from being overwhelmed by more "populist" activities. And general education may need its own enclaves, as in the liberal arts colleges, to avoid being subjugated to either technical training or research. Some activities require their own differentiated environments. Such environments can be created within more multipurpose institutions, but it takes very special effort to create them and very special persistence to perpetuate them. We do, however, favor diversity within institutions of substantial size and multiple functions, as well as among institutions.

Differentiation of structures can better lead to differentiation of treatment than can the combination of all functions within a single structure; what were once called "orbits of coercive comparison" (Ross, 1948, Ch. 3) tend to be less coercive among structures than within a single structure. A variety of functions or sets of functions may better be handled by state agencies with a variety of financial formulas than with only one formula; with separate collective agreements than with the identical agreement—community colleges and research universities are quite different types of institutions; with different admissions policies for students and appointment policies for faculty members than with the same policies; and with different curricular and degree requirement policies than with the same policies, among other examples. Different functions and combinations of functions deserve different treatment, and this is more likely to be forthcoming in separate institutions than in a series of all-encompassing institutions; there are likely to be fewer Procrustean beds. The campus is inherently a multipurpose institution; but it is not necessarily an all-purpose institution. We would thus have grave doubts about the wisdom of creating "comprehensive universities" which include all functions within the same institution.

The research university is a special case. The inclusion of research leads directly to service activities, and it also leads to the training of advanced graduate students, who, in turn, become the teaching assistants for undergraduate students. The research university, consequently, is more of a multipurpose institution than the other types of colleges and universities, but it need not be and should not be an all-purpose institution. There are about 100 research universities in the United States out of 2,800 institutions of all types, and they add their own version of diversity, but the research university type should not become the one and only preferred type. It should be viewed, instead, as a special type with limited applicability. The research university, effectively developed, is very costly and it is worth that cost to society, but it would be very much more costly and not worth the expense to make it the one and only type. The research university is a model, not *the* model; and higher education should not be homogenized around this one model. We regret and would argue against the tendencies of recent years in this direction.

We note that some functions have become intensified in some institutions as well as added to them. The intensification of some functions may be as strong a reason for cutting other functions, as is the addition of new functions.

We have not urged reduction of functions for the sake of a "sense of community." Even rather small and undifferentiated institutions these days tend to have a series of even smaller "communities" within them, as, to a much greater degree, do larger and more differentiated institutions. Few campuses today constitute a single community, in the sense of interaction among all of its members. Few institutions can create such a sense of community no matter what they do about functions.

Public institutions tend to take on more functions than do private institutions since for their political welfare, they need to have more contact with more elements of the public. The private colleges tend to be concerned with fewer constituencies. Thus, the public colleges have the more difficult problem of limiting functions.

Functions may be viewed as "complementary" (and in the research university the complementary functions are comparatively numerous), as competitive for attention and resources, or as essentially independent of other functions. It is our view that complementary functions should be combined, that competitive functions ought to be disaggregated into separate institutions or into separate segments within the same institution, and that independent functions ought to be turned over to other agencies unless there are strong reasons to the contrary. Complementary functions may of course, be combined in many different ways.

Recommendation 22. Institutions of higher education should seek to avoid and to eliminate noncomplementary functions.

Recommendation 23. Coordinating councils, consortia, and multi-campus systems should adopt policies of clear differentiation of functions among campuses and of assigned specializations among fields. Such differentiation of functions should follow the logic of complementarity of interests.

We strongly favor differentiation of functions and specialization of tasks among institutions.

Cohesion

There is, we believe, still another criterion in determining the functions of a campus. This criterion is that nothing should be added if it does not make a contribution to the whole enterprise and something should be subtracted if it would not be missed by the whole enterprise. This is the criterion of cohesiveness, and it goes beyond complementarity.

We believe that many individual institutions of higher education in the United States would be in an improved situation if they were more uniformly concerned with cohesion, in the sense that each function adds to the welfare of the total enterprise. Too often, mere coexistence of functions is accepted—in the sense that different functions, however much in conflict or however disparate or however tangentially related, are carried out under the same name and in the same general location.[2]

Both public understanding and campus unity would be improved if greater cohesion were sought. The function of being almost everything to almost everybody and doing almost anything for almost anybody is no longer sufficient as an academic program. Higher education, generally—and the individual campus, in particular—needs a clearer concept of what it will and will not do. Functions should follow chosen purposes more closely, and the sources of money and power and passion less closely.

Institutions of higher education should eliminate contradictions among their functions (like secret research) and ineffectiveness in the performance of functions—when some other agency can do them as well or better (like purely "company town" activities); and each campus should reduce any incompatibilities among its

---

[2] For a discussion of the "search for internal coherence," see Perkins (1966, Ch. 2).

functions. Each campus should also be able to state what its functions are, why they are important, and how they fit together. It should be able to state why it is a cohesive enterprise.

While we believe that there are reasonable limits to what higher education should try to do in its entirety and to what an individual campus should seek to encompass by way of variety of endeavors, we do not consider these limits to be either crystal clear or uniformly applicable to any and all institutions. And, while we favor efforts at cohesion, we not only acknowledge but even proclaim the advantages of some diversity of effort within as well as among institutions.[3] Research can enrich teaching and vice versa, particularly at the graduate level; science and the humanities in the same institution can make the campus both more interesting to the participants and more vital in its intellectual activities; some conflicts in points of view and methodology can be highly productive. The multipurpose campus can be a more exciting place than a single-purpose institution. We urge adoption of the many golden mean solutions between the extremes of the all-purpose and the single-purpose institution. Our caution is that a campus can do too much as well as too little.

In any event, we do not consider the multiplicity of functions, as do some observers, to have been the one great cause of discontent within higher education in recent years. Such discontent occurred almost equally on smaller and simpler campuses as on larger and more complex ones, and was related more to the type of students and faculty members drawn to each campus than to complexity of functions. Also, the timing of the rise of the discontent and its subsequent reduction were obviously more related to external developments in American society than to the rise and fall of the multiplicity of functions on campus. Since the fall from the state of grace of ancient simplicity did not cause the recent troubles, return to such simplicity could not be expected to bring harmony ever after given the nature of the participating faculty members and students. The combination of functions performed is important but not all-important.

One additional note: higher education should not promise too much. It can contribute substantially to equality of opportunity but only in a minor degree to equality of economic results. It can con-

---

[3] For a discussion of the comparatively high productivity that can result from a "combination of functions" see Ben-David (1971, Ch. 9).

tribute significantly to a higher GNP, but it cannot by itself cause the GNP to rise. It can provide a favorable climate for student development, but it cannot take responsibility for such development; it cannot save souls. It can assist pure scholarship, but it cannot guarantee that the products of such scholarship will add to human happiness. It can provide opportunities for commentary on the conduct of society, but it cannot assure the validity of such commentary; it cannot save the world. It should not promise more than it can reasonably expect to deliver.

Part Three:
Conflict

12. Contending Philosophical Views about Purposes and Functions

The discussion in preceding sections has been concerned (1) with the purposes of higher education in the United States as we view them in the present and for the future in relationship to the needs of individuals and of society more generally (Sections 2 through 8) and (2) with the growth of purposes and functions in the course of American history, and with the operational question of whether or not there is now an overloading of functions as a result of this growth (Sections 9 through 11). We now turn to a new theme of how specific purposes may relate to overall doctrinal views about the central logic of higher education; of how men think about these matters rather than of how they have reacted and should react within actual situations and in response to actual problems.

Three contending views

Three central philosophical views of the primary purposes of learning in general, and of higher learning in particular, have animated men in planning and developing colleges and universities over the centuries. Much of the current intellectual debate about and the struggle over the purposes of higher education has roots, often unnoticed, in these three views.

We set forth these three views as "ideal types," as abstractions from the full reality and complexity of views actually held. We do this in an effort to illuminate the essential philosophical orientations from which more balanced, or at least more mixed, positions are constructed, drawing, as they often do, on elements of two or even all three of these "pure" doctrines—but in quite differing proportions. We fully realize that the policies of many institutions and that the thoughts of many individuals draw on each of these elements to one degree or another; that few institutions and few individuals adhere solely to one unadulterated doctrinal view or the other. The question here, however, is not what all the shades and nuances are that may occur in reality, but what are the primary colors out of which these shades and nuances are combined.

We present these elemental views—these primary tones—for several reasons. First of all, each one of them is important in its own right and the subject of a substantial body of literature. Second, there are real differences among them and great current disagreements among their respective adherents. Third, an appreciation of them individually, and of their intertwining points of conflict and mutual support, can help illuminate the actual debates that take place in faculty clubs, in legislative halls, and in the press; they also illuminate the philosophical bases of actions actually taken. Fourth, each is really an "eternal" point of view and thus the confrontations among them, while rising and falling and taking many different forms at different times and in different places, are likely also to be enduring, are not likely in the near future to fade away forever. Fifth, at any moment of time it is instructive to see how each point of view fares at the interface between the actions in the external society and the internal intellectual dialogue. Many banners are held up, and many different people and different institutions rally now around one and now around another, but each banner is made up in some way from one or more of the primary colors, and can be interpreted with reference to them.

Examined from a purely doctrinal point of view, we do have great controversy in higher education today. This controversy is very difficult for some within and to a few without the campus. The nature and the sources of this philosophical conflict are of interest to many, however, who seek an understanding of the situation and a program for its improvement.

The three views we shall set forth have some overlapping attitudes, as we shall note; but they are not, at their very cores, fully reconcilable with each other, and the resulting doctrinal conflict among their various adherents has recently intensified in the United States. The proponents of the different doctrines, and combinations of doctrines, evaluate the performance of higher education in ways which are quite at odds with each other; and they pull and tug at each other and at higher education as it now exists in the effort to draw it closer each to their own desires. These doctrines and their advocates are a force—albeit not the most determining one—at work on the system.

These three views may be more or less loosely compared with what the Harvard report on the *Nature and Purposes of the Uni-*

versity (Committee on Governance, 1971) calls the *classical* and *pragmatic* models, and, less precisely, identifies as the *political* approach. The terminology of Butts and Cremin for a somewhat parallel classification is *intellectualist, experimentalist* and *reconstructionist* (1953, pp. 496, 497, 545). Related approaches might alternatively be identified as *restorationist, utilitarian,* and *transformational.* By whatever name, and however defined,[1] there are some fundamentally different understandings of the proper central logic of higher education.

What are the principal philosophical alternatives? Which is dominant in the United States today? Has higher education in the United States responded more to doctrine or more to the surrounding society?

Searching for values

The essence of this view is that there are eternal truths in the universe or ultimate values which have been discovered or which can be discovered, that there is an eternal world behind the changing perceptions of the actual world. These truths or values may be found through reason and often, in practice, are related basically to concepts of social justice and of social order. Or they may be found through the revelation of some faith, and may be related to an afterlife as well as to the relations of men on earth. Or they may be found through an amalgamation of both traditions—reason and faith; this is what has been called the "Hellenistic-Christian" tradition. Or they may be found through observation of what works and through intuitive sensations.

Classical humanistic writings and divine texts—great books—embodying those truths already discovered are one primary basis for learning as are reflective and revelatory documents. The effort is to discover, by one means or another, what is true and right for all men at all times and in all places, and then to inculcate these truths and moral judgments in other men and in succeeding generations of men—"the best which has been thought and said in the world" (Arnold, 1871 in 1971, p. 5). There is a belief in an ordered or at least potentially just universe—ordered by natural laws or by

---

[1] Merle Curti speaks of "education to perpetuate the existing pattern of economic and social arrangements; education to modify or reform the established system; and education to completely reorganize affairs in such a way that a future differing fundamentally from the past and present may be achieved." (1935, intro.). Whitehead speaks of the differing approaches "of unity, of multitude, of transition" (1938, p. 116).

divine wisdom or by human reflection on and revelation about value systems.

The philosophers, the religious leaders, and the humanists have the duty to continue the great dialogue, to find the principles, and to teach them to all men. This has been and is the great vision of many highly civilized men; and many students of today demonstrate a resurgence of interest in the continuing search for basic values. What is man's fate? By what values should he govern his conduct?

Pursuing new knowledge

Truth, from this next point of view, is more related to current facts, including facts about the physical universe, and is always being discovered and tested and applied anew. It will be found, in an expanding and changing universe, through analysis of current experience and through experimentation. Bacon wrote about "The Advancement of Learning" and Benjamin Franklin started a society for "Promoting and Propagating Useful Knowledge," which later merged into the American Philosophical Society, each in support of this general approach. William James also supported this general view. As Commager has said, "For James believed, passionately, that truth was not something that was formed, once and for all, but was forever in the making, that it was not single and absolute but plural and contingent" (1955, p. 101). It is more the search that is eternal, and not so much the accepted truths or values. Thus it is change that is constant and not the ordered universe—"all is flux" (Heraclitus, bk. IX, sec. VIII). Or it may be said that there is an eternal clash of opposites, now unifying, now in conflict. There are no unchallenged absolutes. The perspective is more the present, and the recent past and the near future as related to it.

The laboratory takes its place along with the library and the chapel and the discussion group. The purpose of learning is not so much to reinforce or to find the moral precepts and intellectual bulwarks of a more value-oriented society. Rather, it is to devote itself to "the improvement of man's lot" in a society traveling upward, by way of scientific discovery, on the road called Progress. And man's lot may vary—almost certainly will vary—from time to time and from place to place. The scientist and the scholar have the task of finding out how to improve man's lot at each time and in each place, and of sharing their findings with all who may benefit from them. "In natural philosophy, practical results are not only the means to improve human well-being. They are also the guarantee of truth. There is a true rule in religion, that a man must show faith by his works. The same rule holds good in natural philosophy. Science too must be known by its works. It is by the witness of works rather than by logic or even observation that truth is revealed and established. It follows from this that the improvement of man's lot and the improvement of man's mind are one and the same thing."[2] This has been and is the realistic program of many idealistic but also pragmatic men.

Supporting a designated social structure

The starting point for this philosophical approach is one particular envisioned perfected society whether anarchy, or democracy, or the socialist state, or the "cultural revolution" triumphant, or whatever. Anarchy requires the "de-schooling" of society. Democracy, as seen by Jefferson, requires the broad education of the people and the high education of an "aristocracy of talent." Russian Communism has emphasized technical skills and Marxist-Leninist ideology. The "cultural revolution" means to some the cultivation of the sensate, and to others of political awareness — "politics shall take charge." Educational philosophy starts with a blueprint of the desired future for society as a whole.

This has led to the manifestos of many men searching in the past and today for the one and only new Golden Age.

Political and social goals are more important than the library, the chapel, or the laboratory. The good society is not to be found so much in the natural laws of the universe or in man's individual sense of values or in constantly new knowledge and higher skills, but in the determined will of men of convictions about the best social structure. Education is, above all, an instrument of man's will, and the essence of any educational system is determined by those whose will is supreme — the will of the members of which social class or which political party or which philosophical group.

Since there are many visions of the perfected social structure, there are many concepts of what education should be and should do. Among current contending versions are the "de-schooling of society" on the way toward a more decentralized and participatory democracy or anarchy, and training grounds for revolutionary

[2] See Francis Bacon, "Thoughts and Conclusions," quoted in Farrington, 1951, p. 68.

change on the way into some form of communism, among many others. Because visions of the best social structure are so diverse, versions of what higher education ought to be are also quite various.

A tie to current reality is a unifying force for the second school of thought (pursuit of knowledge); and the limited number of cultural models that have survived out of the past or have been created in the present reduces the competition within the first school of thought (search for values), but man's almost unlimited imagination gives great latitude to visions of the correctly designated social structure—and thus to the proper nature of education.

Some social structures will be in effect and subject to attempted preservation by higher education (as in Russia), and some will be in contention and the subject of attempted replacement for the status quo by some within higher education.

The three views compared and contrasted

It should quickly be noted that there are great tensions within each of these three points of view, as well as among them, and that each is really an axis of thought with terminal points quite far apart. There are great differences, for example, between Aquinas and Confucius about values; between Bacon and Franklin about the desired purity of scientific research; and between anarchists and Maoists about social structure. Each approach has its own continuum of points of view. In the case of the second (pursuit of knowledge) the continuum, discipline by discipline, goes from pure "learning" to "useful" applied research, from the theoretical mathematician to the applied engineer. At the extremes they may look like the opposites of each other, and in some ways they are in terms of this axis. But, putting all the in-between gradations together, there is a continuum from the most pure to the most applied, and back again; there are contacts up and down the same continuum in terms of literature read and the personalities known to each other—a chain of connections, a hierarchy of accomplishment. The pure scientists may be more withdrawn from the world and the engineers more immersed within it, but it is the same world; and both are rational, experimental, and innovative in their approach to it. Each derives out of much the same historical tradition, and they talk about the same general order of things, and they fight about the same new developments.

The really big gaps are between and among the three points of view. They do not form a continuum with each other with minor gradations from point to point. They do not grow out of the same historical traditions. There is more similarity of approach *within* each point of view than there is *among* points of view. The way people identify themselves is indicative. Those most concerned with values follow "schools" of thought; those most concerned with knowledge divide themselves by disciplines (disciplines only arose in colleges in the United States when the pursuit of knowledge became the central theme); and those most concerned with Utopian social structures identify themselves by their adherence to one or another political movement.

Higher education can have as its inner logic a search for values, or the pursuit of knowledge, or the creation of a new social structure (and perhaps other central goals as well), or a combination of any two or all three. But its choice (or the choice made for it) about inner logic will have a great impact both on what it does and how it does it.

These three views have not been presented in a logical, philosophical order. Rather, they have been presented in the general order in which they have arisen to prominence on a substantial scale in the history of the United States. The first was especially prominent in the early colonial days; the second assumed dominance over the past century; and the third has attained greater influence in more recent times. But elements of all three views can be found at nearly all times and in many persons. Jefferson, for example, advanced the first (natural laws), the second (science), and the third (democracy).

These different world views show up on campus. The first, in one form or another, tends to find its greatest support in theology, in the humanities, and in the liberal arts college; the second, in one form or another, in the sciences and the professions, and in the land-grant university, the community college, and the comprehensive college; and the third, in one form or another, in some of the social sciences and in the "free universities." The first view tends to emphasize the library and the discussion group; the second, the laboratory and the field trip; and the third, the political platform and off-campus social action.

Two of these views, the first (values) and the third (social structure) are more nearly like each other in their inherent logic of a more stabilized orientation toward a set of values or a designated social structure than they are like the second (knowledge) which is more oriented to means and less to ends. They are also more like each other in certain other ways: neither is dominant in higher educatic in the United States today, and thus both are "outs" attacking th "in" of "pursuit of knowledge." Thus they both criticize the secor and often in much the same terms—lack of clear principles, to much service to the existing society, addiction to constant, sma and allegedly inconsequential adjustments—even though they a not basically compatible with each other in a number of other way They both quite naturally emphasize the "critical" function higher education as against the more supportive approach of th second view toward society. They both look down upon the alleg crudities of current practice, the one from the vantage point humanistic values and the other from the vantage point of the tru "good" society.

But all three views also have certain concerns in common. The all believe that the higher learning should be useful for some pu pose or purposes; that the higher learning should be concerned wi the "truth," though variously defined and variously discovere and that higher education should lead to change in one direction another and by one means or another. Thus education is seen be each as a high activity of man and as an instrument that can he shape a better world.

The stronger proponents of each point of view, however, share basic skepticism about and sometimes even hostility toward ea other. Proponents of the first general view believe that the followe of the second view have often led higher education from the heigh of pure scholarship into the market place where service is boug and sold—as having lost the faith; they believe that the proponen of the third view would take it by force into the streets and sta building barricades. Proponents of the second view look at the fi school as out of tune with reality, and at the third school as esse tially anti-intellectual and bent on internal conflict and exterr repression. And proponents of the third school view the other tw as supporters of outmoded social systems—as having never fou the true faith; and supporters of the second school, in particular, "mandarins" of the status quo.

A second crosscut—individualism versus centralism

It is also important to set forth a second crosscut view of high education. This crosscut is by the degree of emphasis placed up societal control and interests as compared with decisions by indivi uals and the interests of individuals. Thus values can be express

CHART 1 *Orientations of higher education*

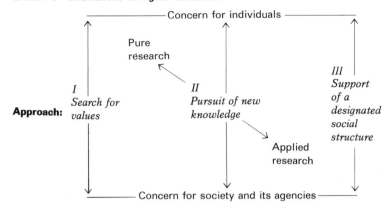

through authoritarian control or through "rugged individualism"; the point of view of evolutionary knowledge, through centralized planning or individual initiative—"bureaucratic centralism" versus competitive and cooperative participation; and the nature of a perfected social structure, through anarchism or state socialism. With this crosscut added, it might then be better to say that there are six "ideal-type" approaches rather than three.

Another way of stating this crosscut is to ask whether the values or the knowledge or the social structure is intended more to serve the society as a whole or the individual members of it or some combination of the two. This crosscut of orientation toward society or toward the individual fits better the approaches of "values" and of "social structure" than it does of "new knowledge" which is more likely, in principle, to be directed toward both. The more important crosscut for the "new knowledge" approach is according to whether the approach is pure or applied. (See Chart I.)

An illustration of the importance of this crosscut is the shift in research emphasis in the United States after World War II to federal concerns in general and to defense concerns in particular, and from reliance on state, foundation, and private funds to greater reliance on the single source of the federal government. This was a massive shift, with many consequences, on the axis that connects national and individual interests. And the federal government has, in turn, shifted back and forth on the axis that connects basic and applied research—currently it favors applied research. Major elements of higher education have become more dependent on and even more a part of the mechanisms of political and economic power.

The three views in actual conflict

Each view has experienced its periods of triumph. The first vie
generally ruled supreme in Western Europe at least until the end
the sixteenth century; the second view rose gradually to dominanc
particularly in the nineteenth century; and the third view has bee
gaining strength in the twentieth century. The world of earlier ce
turies was more compatible with the first outlook; the newer wor
of science and technology and geographic and anthropologic
discoveries, with the second; and the modernized world, with i
greater alternatives held in the hands of men as a result of tl
economic and political and educational revolutions, might turn o
in the end to be more compatible with the third, and, perhaps, al:
with the first.

In the history of higher learning in the Western world, ve
broadly viewed, first came a particular devotion to a search f
values, and then a contest between the concern for values and tl
rising theme of evolutionary knowledge; this was followed by tl
dominance of evolutionary knowledge but with strong attention
values continuing in some areas. Now there has arisen a new co
test between evolutionary knowledge and visions of a perfecte
social structure with a regenerated interest in the validity of tl
pursuit of values as an alternative approach—which is where v
stand in America today and in much of the world.

Fundamental purpose is once again in open dispute in the Unite
States. Once the question was the teaching of morality—the o
style *in loco parentis* drew on a then-established system of valu
versus the newer scientific research method; now it is the old
"objectivity" versus the newer political commitment and "visiona
imagination"; once it was inherited or ascribed class status vers
equality of opportunity for the young, now it is competitive merit
cracy versus equality of academic results; once it was the "who
man" versus the occupational expert, now it is the occupation
expert versus political man; once it was the man of faith versus tl
inner-directed man of action, now it is the inner-directed expe
versus the peer group-oriented activist; once it was service to tl
church, the state, and the ancient professions versus service
agriculture and industry and the common man, now it is servi
to the society in existence versus service to a society that son
people want to see born; once it was the classics versus the "mo
ern" subjects, now it is the modernized curriculum versus tl
ideological or the sensate.

Once again battles are being fought on a broad front as they were, in the United States, particularly from 1870 to 1910.[3] From the perspective of history, the outcome of that earlier battle was clear—the diverse forces of science and of populist democracy were so overwhelming, with the former pressing for better knowledge and the latter for the wider distribution and appreciation of knowledge. But the outcome of the new battle is not, as yet, so clear— although the pursuit of knowledge for individuals and society remains the dominant approach today.

Around the world, similar confrontations are taking place in a number of countries, although in a few a single philosophy has exclusive official support. But in the world of international scholarship it is largely the second view of evolutionary knowledge that creates the basis for contacts and for cooperation. The other views have elements of divisiveness and absolutism in them that hinder universality of discussion; they each lead more toward particularism. Thus science and technology are among the most international of fields. To the extent that a world society of intellectual endeavor is forming, it is more likely to continue along this path of attempted understanding of and alternative solutions to practical problems than along the path of either of the other major alternative routes, each of which lends itself to being exclusive and authoritarian in point of view.

To a degree, though perhaps a lesser degree, all of American society—even most industrialized societies—and not just higher education alone, faces a new debate over purposes, a new struggle over goals. To some extent this is probably also true for many individuals in and outside of academic life: a concern (1) for what can realistically be accomplished at the moment, (2) for the framework of values within which the accomplishments are sought, and (3) for the "good" structure toward which such accomplishments may lead or at least with which they are not considered inconsistent.

Earlier we set forth our convictions about the five major purposes of higher education for the present and for the period ahead. These convictions were based on our views of the changes now going on in society and on campus. We also drew on each of the three philosophical views we have set forth. Our emphasis, for example, on the importance of "academic socialization" and on general educa-

---

[3] "One's academic allegiance" was determined by one's views of "basic purpose" in this conflict. (Veysey, 1965, p. viii).

tion draws on values; our stress on "advancing human capability" draws on the approach of evolutionary knowledge; and our concern for effective "evaluation of society" through individual study and comment draws on the philosophical concept of helping to shape a better future. Our main approach, however, has been that of the evolution of knowledge and how it can be advanced most successfully, of the application of free and trained thought and research to the great problems of the current age.

We have also considered the comparative emphasis to be placed upon individuals and on society. This Commission has generally tended to favor the individual rather than the collective approach to higher education, whenever the two are reasonable alternatives to each other, as expressed in its support of institutional independence, of academic freedom, of distribution of federal funds and through students, of federal support of research through individual projects evaluated on a competitive basis, of adjustment to the labor market through student choice rather than by manpower planning, of more academic options open to students, and of alternative channels into life and work. We have placed reliance more on the free choice of individuals among alternatives available to them rather than on centralized collective determinations, have declared faith in our respect for the decision-making capacity of individual persons.

The impacts of doctrine and of surrounding society

We now turn to the question of whether the actual purposes of higher education as they have developed in the United States have responded more to contending philosophical orientations or to the changing nature of society. We identified four purposes that have evolved in America: personal development, economic growth, political health, and service; these can be translated, in part, into the five purposes we see for the present and for the future.

The purpose of personal development has drawn on the first view of the importance of moral values, but more in earlier times than today. The purposes of economic growth and of service to society have relied more on the second view of contributions to new knowledge and increasingly so. The purpose of political health in a democratic society has made contact, in part, with the third view of contributions to some more perfected society.

The practice of higher education, however, has been more connected with the nature of the surrounding society than with doctrines of any single philosophical view. Higher education has responded more to the expressed needs of individual Americans and of American society than to any body of theory. It has found such consistency as it has had in a more or less parallel relationship to society. In paralleling American society, it has drawn on all three theories, and this has led to the doctrinal conflict noted earlier. The practical conflict would have been greater, however, if there had been doctrinal clarity throughout and a consequent major inconsistency with the diverse aspects of a changing and pluralistic society.[4]

The specific origins of American society in the Western Europe of the seventeenth century encouraged attention in higher education to moral values. The political and industrial revolutions that America later experienced gave great impetus to the point of view of the evolution of knowledge. The more recent educational revolution of mass attendance, the many problems of a postindustrial society, and the rise of new mentalities each help to accentuate the emphasis placed by some on the perfected society.

There are at least two good reasons why contending theoretical schools have not had more of an impact on higher education in the contemporary United States. (1) To begin with, the United States is a pluralistic society, and adherence exclusively to the doctrines of any one school—particularly the first and the third—would cause higher education to be in great dissonance with society. (2) Additionally, it is not the nature of the intellectual world, without great external control, to agree totally on one cultural model, on one mentality, as against all others—and the external control to force such agreement is not present in American society. The past, the present, and the future are all of interest to the free-flowing intellectual world; also deduction, induction, and inspiration; also cultural elitism and meritocratic expertise; and so forth. One mentality may be ascendant but not to the total exclusion of all others. American society is pluralistic, and the inherent nature of the intellectual world is such that it also is pluralistic. Thus all three schools have been and will continue to be in contention as far as one can see

---

[4] As early as the Revolution, American education at all levels was responding to pressures from diverse groups. "In the last analysis, it seemed less important to maintain traditional definitions of education than it did to accommodate those who desired it. Virtually anyone could teach and virtually anyone could learn, at least among whites, and the market rather than the church or the legislature governed through multifarious contractual relationships." (Cremin, 1970, p. 559).

ahead. Doctrinal purity in the approach to higher education in the United States is highly unlikely.

Higher education has followed, in large part, the great changes in American society. This is not to suggest, however, a theory of strict societal determinism but rather that the surrounding society has been the major single determinant at work. Many other forces have also been at work—philosophical theories being one. The sphere of thought has, inherently, a major degree of autonomy, and follows its own laws of development. We recognize that higher education may lag behind society, as it did to some extent in the United States before the Civil War; may isolate itself from society, as in some medieval monasteries; may oppose society, as do some elements in some universities in Latin America; or it may generally match changes in society, as in the United States since the Civil War. Higher education in the United States remains today a subsystem of the society and is just as likely to be greatly affected by how that society develops in the future as it has been in the past. And, in particular, as American society becomes even more complex, the purposes of higher education are also likely to become even more complex; as American society becomes more controversial, higher education also becomes controversial only more so—when the United States quivers, higher education quakes.

The period of great change in American society around 1870 became a period of great change for higher education; and a great philosophical debate about higher education then took place. To the extent that the period of 1970 turns out to be a period of great change for American society, we expect that it will be one also for higher education and that a major philosophical debate will again take place. A debate about purposes is always endemic in higher education. Under some societal circumstances it becomes epidemic. We consider in our concluding section, which follows, the possibility that this may be such a time.

13. The Future—A Period of Conflict about Purposes and Functions?

The always latent and long-standing debate about the purposes of higher education is now being invigorated. American society is once again changing rapidly. Public attitudes about higher education are less supportive, more questioning. New tensions exist on campus and between campus and society.

More faculty members, and students, want to use the campus as a direct instrument of social change. At the same time that this new challenge of commitment is being mounted, an older view of academic withdrawal from direct involvement with society is once again being advanced. The status quo of "objective" participation in society through the creation of knowledge and addition to skills is under attack from two directions on campus. What is the most likely outcome?

Higher education left to its own devices, its own internal interests and mechanisms, has seldom in history changed its basic structures and policies and purposes except by slow accretion of small decisions. The content of many of the different fields of learning (and thus of courses of instruction), however, has changed quite dramatically, particularly through application of the concept of evolutionary knowledge. Major changes, this one important exception aside, have generally reflected changes in society and in the impact of society on campus. It is always possible, of course, despite the historical record, that some internal group may gain control of higher education and change it basically in terms of its purposes; but this would be a rare event.

Thus two factors are of crucial importance in assessing how fast and how far higher education in the United States may change its purposes and functions in the future.

1   The first factor is whether higher education on its own, quite contrary to most of past history, might seek to take off in some new

direction, aside from the changing content of particular subject matter fields. An effort to return to an emphasis on values may be viewed as an attempt to loosen the ties to society and thus to reduce the prospect for change in the long run; to continue with evolutionary knowledge as the predominant view, as an acceptance of change along with society and of a modest effort to change society at the same time that society is changing higher education; and to opt for an action approach to a designated future society, as an adventure in trying to shape society—not be shaped by it, according to some one vision or another; and to greatly speed up the process of internal change in the course of getting ready for this adventure.

We consider that the most likely outcome will be a continuation of the basic approach—subject to continuing modifications—that has dominated since 1870; that means moving along with American society and, in some aspects, ahead of it in a relatively loose interaction. No major challenge is likely to come from an effort to return to an emphasis on values—the supporters of that point of view have been largely accommodated within the existing system of higher education, although they are often highly critical of it, and can be accommodated additionally within it if more faculty members and more students want to follow this approach. The challenge of greater import is coming from the proponents of a designated future society approach, not because their theoretical arguments have recently become necessarily any different or any better than in the past, but, rather, because our society is increasingly future-oriented, man has more possibilities of shaping his own future, and intellectuals with imaginative mentalities are more numerous. The pull of the future, the new openness of society to the will of man as against the dictates of nature, the rise of the "new class" of intellectuals in numbers and in positions of influence, all make alternative cultural models more attractive on campus as compared with acceptance of the slowly changing status quo. This challenge is largely an internal one for there is as yet no major constituency in the general public which supports it—quite the contrary.

2   The second factor is how closely higher education is tied to society and the extent to which society changes its formal and informal inputs into higher education, as through more or less research funds, or more or different students, or added controls and policies, or new problems presented to higher education for help in solution.

The closer the tie to society and the greater the change in the inputs from society, the more higher education is likely to change. The looser the tie and the smaller the change in inputs, the less higher education is likely to change.

Public authority in recent times has been substantially strengthening its ties to higher education by adding to its control and influence. In the struggle over the future directions of higher education, society is increasing its control and interjecting its policies more vigorously. Although some elements of higher education, some enclaves within it, will seek to fight society not for the sake of higher education but for the sake of capturing society and guiding it in different directions, we expect these efforts largely to fail.

Between these two efforts—one to break the ties, the other to tighten them—it is our belief that the second is the more powerful force, and, in fact, that the first effort may only add to the strength of the second effort.

Thus, it becomes quite important how American society may change and also how it may change its inputs into higher education. No one can really know the answer as yet. However, it does appear to us that the United States will continue on its meritocratic-humane course: a meritocratic approach to the production of goods and services and to the selection of political, social, intellectual, and artistic leadership, and a more humane approach to redistribution of opportunity, income, and services increasingly on a more egalitarian basis. The five purposes of higher education for the foreseeable future, as we have set them forth above, are generally consistent with this general direction for society.

If the ties between society and higher education do become stronger and not weaker, and if American society continues to move in the direction that we have indicated, and thus is not heading for a revolution led by the academics as we are convinced it is not, then how higher education as a whole (and society) will react to the inevitable continuing efforts of some within higher education to move both higher education and society in quite new directions becomes quite important. We expect a continuation of the current conflict between the two cultural approaches to higher education of pursuing the evolution of knowledge on the one hand (with the reluctant support in this battle of the proponents of a more value-centered approach) and of promoting a designated future society through action on the other. We expect that the intensity of this conflict will rise and fall. We believe that it is of the greatest importance, however, that some effective "rules of the game" be worked out soon within higher education and with society to govern this conflict; otherwise higher education will be subject to being unduly disrupted internally, or partially abandoned and increasingly controlled externally, or both. It is for this reason that we have elsewhere proposed an "Academic Constitution" (Carnegie Commission on Higher Education, 1972a) and a "Bill of Rights and Responsibilities" (Carnegie Commission on Higher Education, 1971c).

Intellectuals, with their major home on campus, are increasingly numerous in an advanced industrial nation such as our own, are often concentrated in self-confirming groups and in constant contact with each other, and hold more essential positions in society than in most earlier times. They are a new force of production but are, to some extent and at the same time, critical of the existing system of production; they adhere in substantial numbers to the "adversary culture" (Trilling, 1965). As we have noted earlier, about one-fifth to one-third of faculty members would now appear, to one degree or another, to be associated with the "adversary culture." Thus, a "collision course" (Riesman, 1969) is inevitable between elements of the intelligentsia, including elements on campus, and elements of the larger society for this and for other reasons. The campus, almost of necessity, is one point of collision, as in Germany today (Schelsky, 1972). Since the campus is at least intermittently involved in the confrontation of these partially contradictory forces, it needs to be quite clear what role it will play. The likely long-term decline in the comparative income of the intellectual working force can only make the role of the university a more difficult one because of the intensified impact of this prospective decline on the tension that basically already exists.

How may the purposes of higher education, as we see them as the United States approaches the year 2000, be affected by these developments of a closer tie between higher education and society, of a changing American society with changing inputs into higher education, and of an internal dispute over the orientation of higher education to society?

We see no special problems for the continuation of "pure scholarship" provided academic freedom is protected against internal and external attacks upon it, and a reasonable supply of resources is available.

We see no especially new problems for the purposive effort of higher education to advance human capability throughout society. These efforts will be actively supported by society and will probably continue to be reasonably well performed.

The educational advancement of students will need to be more responsive, in particular, to the changing labor market situation. The developmental growth of students, as we have noted, is an area with many unknowns. The problem of working with the "sliders" will be particularly difficult. Here again, much debate will take place and many experiments will be tried.

Educational justice will need to be served more effectively and this can only be done as more preferred channels, in addition to college as the one and only preferred channel, to adult life are opened up, and as the principle of a "youth endowment" for many uses replaces subsidies for the college-bound alone. Otherwise the pressures on college attendance will be too great; there will be too many reluctant attenders; there will be too great a sense of injustice as between those who do not and those who do receive subsidies; and the labor market will be unduly burdened with college graduates.

We do see a coming contest between supporters of equality of opportunity and those who favor, rather, equality of academic and economic results. The long-time efforts at equality of opportunity are just beginning to show dramatic returns on the effort expended when a new battle is being joined on behalf of equality of results. This battle is already evidencing itself in conflict over many aspects of academic life, such as admission policies, differentiation of functions, grading practices, employment and promotion of faculty members, awarding of degrees. This almost across-the-board conflict in orientation is bound to continue and even intensify over the long run.

There will be a continuing struggle over the philosophy of higher education as it faces society—should it support and change society, or should it only seek to change it? We set aside both the possibility of withdrawal into isolation and the possibility of purely submissive service. We do expect the purpose of critical evaluation, under the current social circumstances, to become more important than in the past. How constructive this effort may be and how well higher education and society may work out the rules of the game will be essential questions as higher education faces its future. We have earlier suggested the general principles which we believe should govern the conduct of this function. They call, among other things, for individual academic freedom, for essential institutional independence, and for individual and institutional restraint in the area of direct political and social action. We believe that the conduct of this purpose, above all others, will be the one most involved in internal and external controversy.

Thus a conflict over purposes does exist—more in connection with some purposes than others. We believe that elements of this controversy will confront higher education for the rest of this century at least. The main issue in contention will be whether or not higher education, in whole or in part, should become a base for action against society on behalf of one or another vision of a designated future society. Another overarching issue will be the place in consideration and in decision making given to the individual as compared with the place given to the institution and to government. These two issues involve a different series of considerations and different sets of contestants.

Specific subjects of controversy will include, we believe, disputes (1) over the proper attention to be given to the developmental growth of students, including "sliders," (2) over equality of educational opportunity versus equality of academic results, (3) over the employment of members of minority groups and of women on faculties, and (4) over direct participation of institutions of higher education in political controversies and over the tactics of those who favor such participation.

We have indicated our positions on each of these four issues: for more concern about the quality of the campus environment within which developmental growth takes place and against total campus responsibility for individual developmental growth; for equality of educational opportunity and against equality of academic results; for special consideration of members of minority groups and of women for faculty positions within an enlarged definition of excellence of the academic environment in its totality; and for protection of individual opportunities to engage in the evaluation of society through thought and persuasion and against direct institutional involvement in this activity. Our stand on the fourth issue also means that we oppose efforts to turn the campus into a base for political action against society. Our stand on many issues supports a strong place for the individual in the decision-making process.

A period of temporary quiescence, after the stormy period from 1964 to 1970, should not delude us into thinking that these and other issues have disappeared forever in the future. There may even be again some incandescent situations like that of May 1970. There will be much intermittent controversy. There will be some substantial modifications of purposes and functions. However, there will be no academic revolution affecting the central logic of higher education as generally operative in the United States.

Higher education is a part of society and not totally apart from it. It draws on society and also adds to it. The quality of these reciprocal relationships is of great importance in a society where the system of higher education has substantial independence, and where new knowledge and higher skills are increasingly important to the welfare of society.

The broad alternatives for higher education are to try to withdraw from societal conduct, to participate in society, or to fight society as now constituted. The course of effective participation, we believe, holds out the greater prospects both for higher education and for American society. "A university should reflect the spirit of the times, without yielding to it,"[1] as Lord Bryce once commented. It is *in* but not totally *of* society. It should be more than a mirror but less than a whip. This in-between role places it in an inherently exposed and hazardous position.

The broad alternatives for society are to dispense with much of higher education, to work along with it, or to control it in detail. The course of working along with higher education, we believe, also holds out the better prospects.

Higher education and American society should join in support of the purposes of advancing the educational and developmental growth of students, enlarging human capability throughout society, enhancing educational justice, forwarding pure scholarship, and assisting critical evaluation of society within reasonable rules of the game.

The United States has what is, in many ways, the vanguard system of higher education in the world. How it resolves its problems related to its purposes and functions is, thus, of concern even beyond its own confines.

Higher education should serve society by serving the cause of knowledge; should serve the cause of knowledge by protecting the freedom of its members and the essential independence of its institutions (Carnegie Commission on Higher Education, 1973); and should protect freedom and independence by responding with consideration to the needs of society and by safeguarding its own universal values of free thought and expression.

---

[1] Quoted in Frederick Jackson Turner, "Pioneer Ideals and The State University," commencement address at the University of Indiana, 1910 (Turner, 1962, p. 284).

References

Arnold, Matthew: *Culture and Anarchy,* The Bobbs-Merrill Company, Inc., Indianapolis, 1971. (First published in 1871.)

Ashby, Eric: *Technology and the Academics: An Essay on Universities and the Scientific Revolution,* Macmillan & Co., Ltd., London, 1959.

Ashby, Eric: "The Future of the Nineteenth Century Idea of a University," *Minerva,* vol. 6, pp. 3–17, Autumn 1967.

Ashby, Eric: "A Hippocratic Oath for the Academic Profession," *Minerva,* vol. 8, pp. 64–66, Autumn-Winter 1968–69.

Ashby, Eric, and Mary Anderson: *The Rise of the Student Estate in Britain,* Harvard University Press, Cambridge, Mass., 1970.

Beard, Charles A.: *The Unique Function of Education in American Society,* National Education Association, Washington, D.C., 1937.

Becker, Gary S.: *Human Capital: A Theoretical and Empirical Analysis, with Special Reference to Education,* National Bureau of Economic Research, general series no. 80, Columbia University Press, New York, 1964.

Bell, Daniel: "By Whose Right," in Harold Hodgkinson and L. Richard Meeth (eds.), *Power and Authority,* Jossey-Bass, Inc., Publishers, San Francisco, 1971.

Ben-David, Joseph: *The Scientist's Role in Society: A Comparative Study,* Prentice-Hall, Inc., Englewood Cliffs, N.J., 1971.

Boyd, Julian P. (ed.): *The Papers of Thomas Jefferson,* vol. 9, Princeton University Press, Princeton, N.J., 1950, *et seq.*

Brubacher, John A., and Willis Rudy: *Higher Education in Transition: A History of American Colleges and Universities, 1636–1968,* Harper & Row, Publishers, Incorporated, New York, 1968.

Butts, R. Freeman, and Lawrence A. Cremin: *A History of Education in American Culture,* Holt, Rinehart and Winston, Inc., New York, 1953.

Carnegie Commission on Higher Education: *Quality and Equality: New Levels of Federal Responsibility for Higher Education,* McGraw-Hill Book Company, New York, 1968.

Carnegie Commission on Higher Education: *National Survey of Faculty and Student Opinion,* directed by Martin Trow, Berkeley, Calif., 1969. (Unpublished.)

Carnegie Commission on Higher Education: *A Chance to Learn: An Action Agenda for Equal Opportunity in Higher Education,* McGraw-Hill Book Company, New York, 1970a.

Carnegie Commission on Higher Education: *Quality and Equality: Revised Recommendations,* McGraw-Hill Book Company, New York, 1970b.

Carnegie Commission on Higher Education: *The Capitol and the Campus: State Responsibility for Postsecondary Education,* McGraw-Hill Book Company, New York, 1971a.

Carnegie Commission on Higher Education: *New Students and New Places: Policies for the Future Growth and Development of American Higher Education,* McGraw-Hill Book Company, New York, 1971b.

Carnegie Commission on Higher Education: *Dissent and Disruption: Proposals for Consideration by the Campus,* McGraw-Hill Book Company, New York, 1971c.

Carnegie Commission on Higher Education: *Reform on Campus: Changing Students, Changing Academic Programs,* McGraw-Hill Book Company, New York, 1972a.

Carnegie Commission on Higher Education: *The Campus and the City: Maximizing Assets and Reducing Liabilities,* McGraw-Hill Book Company, New York, 1972b.

Carnegie Commission on Higher Education: *Institutional Aid: Federal Support to Colleges and Universities,* McGraw-Hill Book Company, New York, 1972c.

Carnegie Commission on Higher Education: *Governance of Higher Education: Six Priority Problems,* McGraw-Hill Book Company, New York, 1973.

Carnegie Commission on Higher Education: *Technical Notes on Purposes and Performance in Higher Education,* forthcoming.

Commager, Henry Steele: *The American Mind,* Yale University Press, New Haven, Conn., 1955.

Committee on Governance, Harvard University: *The Nature and Purposes of the University,* Cambridge, Mass., 1971.

Cremin, Lawrence: *American Education: The Colonial Experience, 1607–1783,* Harper & Row, Publishers, Incorporated, New York, 1970.

Curti, Merle: *The Social Ideas of American Educators,* Charles Scribner's Sons, New York, 1935.

Denison, Edward F.: *Why Growth Rates Differ,* The Brookings Institution, Washington, D.C., 1967.

Farrington, Benjamin: *Francis Bacon: Philosopher of Industrial Science,* Lawrence and Wishart, London, 1951.

Faure, Edgar, et al.: *Learning to Be: The World of Education Today and Tomorrow,* UNESCO, Paris, 1972.

Fine, Nathan: *Labor and Farmer Parties in the United States, 1828–1928,* Russell & Russell, New York, 1961.

Gardner, John W.: *Self-Renewal: The Individual and the Innovative Society,* Harper & Row, Publishers, Incorporated, New York, 1963.

Griliches, Z.: "Research Expenditures, Education, and the Aggregate Agricultural Production Function," *American Economic Review,* vol. 54, pp. 961–974, December 1964.

Handlin, Oscar, and Mary F. Handlin: *The American College and American Culture: Socialization as a Function of Higher Education,* McGraw-Hill Book Company, New York, 1970.

Heraclitus: *Diogenes Laertius,* bk. IX, sec. VIII.

Hofstadter, Richard, and Walter P. Metzger: *The Development of Academic Freedom in the United States,* Columbia University Press, New York, 1955.

Hutchins, Robert M.: *The Learning Society,* Frederick A. Praeger, Inc., New York, 1968.

Hutchins, Robert M.: "The Great Anti-School Campaign," in Robert M. Hutchins and Mortimer J. Adler (eds.), *The Great Ideas Today — 1972,* Frederick A. Praeger, Inc., New York, 1972, pp. 154–227.

Juster, F. Thomas, (ed.): *Education, Income, and Human Behavior,* McGraw-Hill Book Company, New York, forthcoming.

Keniston, Kenneth, and Mark Gerzon: "Human and Social Benefits," in American Council on Education, *Universal Higher Education: Costs and Benefits,* background papers for participants in the 1971 annual meeting, Washington, D.C., 1971, pp. 37–62.

Lipset, Seymour M.: *The First New Nation: The United States in Historical and Comparative Perspective,* Basic Books, Inc., Publishers, New York, 1963.

Lipset, Seymour M., and Everett C. Ladd, Jr.: 1972 Faculty Opinion Election Study, reported in "Faculties Divided on Recruiting More Women, Blacks, Chicanos," *Chronicle of Higher Education,* Nov. 13, 1972, pp. 1, 4.

Machlup, Fritz: "European Universities as Partisans," in *Neutrality or Partisanship: A Dilemma of Academic Institutions,* Bulletin no. 34, The Carnegie Foundation for the Advancement of Teaching, New York, 1971, pp. 7–30.

Parsons, Talcott, and Gerald M. Platt: "Age, Social Structure and Socialization in Higher Education," *Sociology of Education,* Winter 1970.

Perkins, James A.: *The University in Transition,* Princeton University Press, Princeton, N.J., 1966.

Riesman, David: "Collision Course of Higher Education," *Journal of College Student Personnel,* November 1969.

Ross, A. M.: *Trade Union Wage Policy,* University of California Press, Berkeley, 1948.

Schelsky, Helmut: "The Wider Setting of Disorder in the German Universities," *Minerva,* pp. 614–626, October 1972.

Spaeth, Joe L., and Andrew M. Greeley: *Recent Alumni and Higher Education,* McGraw-Hill Book Company, New York, 1970.

Trilling, Lionel: *Beyond Culture: Essays on Literature and Learning,* The Viking Press, Inc., New York, 1965.

Trow, Martin: "Reflections on the Transition from Mass to Universal Higher Education," *Daedalus,* vol. 99, pp. 1–43, Winter 1970.

Turner, Frederick Jackson: *The Frontier in American History,* Holt, Rinehart and Winston, Inc., New York, 1962. (Originally published in 1920.)

Van Alstyne, William W.: "The Specific Theory of Academic Freedom and the General Issue of Civil Liberties," *Annals of the American Academy of Political and Social Science,* vol. 404, November 1972.

Veysey, Laurence R.: *The Emergence of the American University,* The University of Chicago Press, Chicago, 1965.

Whitehead, Alfred North: *Modes of Thought,* Cambridge University Press, London, 1938.

Whitehead, Alfred North: *Science and the Modern World,* The Macmillan Company, New York, 1939.

Wilkinson, Rupert: *Gentlemanly Power, British Leadership and Public School Tradition: A Comparative Study in the Making of Rulers,* Oxford University Press, London, 1964.

Withey, Stephen B.: *A Degree and What Else?: Correlates and Consequences of a College Education,* McGraw-Hill Book Company, New York, 1971.

Wolfle, Dael: *The Uses of Talent,* Princeton University Press, Princeton, N.J., 1971.

Wolfle, Dael: *The Home of Science: The Role of the University,* McGraw-Hill Book Company, New York, 1972.

Carnegie Commission on Higher Education
Sponsored Research Studies

BETWEEN TWO WORLDS:
A PROFILE OF NEGRO HIGHER EDUCATION
Frank Bowles and Frank A. DeCosta

BREAKING THE ACCESS BARRIERS:
A PROFILE OF TWO-YEAR COLLEGES
Leland L. Medsker and Dale Tillery

ANY PERSON, ANY STUDY:
AN ESSAY ON HIGHER EDUCATION IN THE
UNITED STATES
Eric Ashby

THE NEW DEPRESSION IN HIGHER
EDUCATION:
A STUDY OF FINANCIAL CONDITIONS AT 41
COLLEGES AND UNIVERSITIES
Earl F. Cheit

FINANCING MEDICAL EDUCATION:
AN ANALYSIS OF ALTERNATIVE POLICIES
AND MECHANISMS
Rashi Fein and Gerald I. Weber

HIGHER EDUCATION IN NINE COUNTRIES:
A COMPARATIVE STUDY OF COLLEGES AND
UNIVERSITIES ABROAD
*Barbara B. Burn, Philip G. Altbach, Clark Kerr,
and James A. Perkins*

BRIDGES TO UNDERSTANDING:
INTERNATIONAL PROGRAMS OF AMERICAN
COLLEGES AND UNIVERSITIES
Irwin T. Sanders and Jennifer C. Ward

GRADUATE AND PROFESSIONAL EDUCATION,
1980:
A SURVEY OF INSTITUTIONAL PLANS
Lewis B. Mayhew

THE AMERICAN COLLEGE AND AMERICAN
CULTURE:
SOCIALIZATION AS A FUNCTION OF HIGHER
EDUCATION
Oscar Handlin and Mary F. Handlin

RECENT ALUMNI AND HIGHER EDUCATION:
A SURVEY OF COLLEGE GRADUATES
Joe L. Spaeth and Andrew M. Greeley

CHANGE IN EDUCATIONAL POLICY:
SELF-STUDIES IN SELECTED COLLEGES AND
UNIVERSITIES
Dwight R. Ladd

STATE OFFICIALS AND HIGHER EDUCATION:
A SURVEY OF THE OPINIONS AND
EXPECTATIONS OF POLICY MAKERS IN NINE
STATES
Heinz Eulau and Harold Quinley

ACADEMIC DEGREE STRUCTURES:
INNOVATIVE APPROACHES
PRINCIPLES OF REFORM IN DEGREE
STRUCTURES IN THE UNITED STATES
Stephen H. Spurr

COLLEGES OF THE FORGOTTEN AMERICANS:
A PROFILE OF STATE COLLEGES AND
REGIONAL UNIVERSITIES
E. Alden Dunham

FROM BACKWATER TO MAINSTREAM:
A PROFILE OF CATHOLIC HIGHER
EDUCATION
Andrew M. Greeley

THE ECONOMICS OF THE MAJOR PRIVATE
UNIVERSITIES
William G. Bowen
(Out of print, but available from University Microfilms.)

THE FINANCE OF HIGHER EDUCATION
Howard R. Bowen
(Out of print, but available from University Microfilms.)

ALTERNATIVE METHODS OF FEDERAL
FUNDING FOR HIGHER EDUCATION
Ron Wolk
(Out of print, but available from University Microfilms.)

INVENTORY OF CURRENT RESEARCH ON
HIGHER EDUCATION 1968
Dale M. Heckman and Warren Bryan Martin
(Out of print, but available from University Microfilms.)

*The following technical reports are available from the Carnegie Commission on Higher Education, 1947
Center Street, Berkeley, California 94704.*

RESOURCE USE IN HIGHER EDUCATION:
TRENDS IN OUTPUT AND INPUTS, 1930–1967
June O'Neill

TRENDS AND PROJECTIONS OF PHYSICIANS
IN THE UNITED STATES 1967–2002
Mark S. Blumberg

MAY 1970:
THE CAMPUS AFTERMATH OF CAMBODIA
AND KENT STATE
Richard E. Peterson and John A. Bilorusky

MENTAL ABILITY AND HIGHER EDUCATIONAL
ATTAINMENT IN THE 20TH CENTURY
Paul Taubman and Terence Wales

AMERICAN COLLEGE AND UNIVERSITY
ENROLLMENT TRENDS IN 1971
Richard E. Peterson

PAPERS ON EFFICIENCY IN THE
MANAGEMENT OF HIGHER EDUCATION
*Alexander M. Mood, Colin Bell,
Lawrence Bogard, Helen Brownlee,
and Joseph McCloskey*

AN INVENTORY OF ACADEMIC INNOVATION
AND REFORM
Ann Heiss

ESTIMATING THE RETURNS TO EDUCATION:
A DISAGGREGATED APPROACH
Richard S. Eckaus

SOURCES OF FUNDS TO COLLEGES AND
UNIVERSITIES
June O'Neill

NEW DEPRESSION IN HIGHER EDUCATION—
TWO YEARS LATER
Earl F. Cheit

PRECARIOUS PROFESSORS: NEW PATTERNS OF REPRESENTATION, by Joseph W. Garbarino, reprinted from INDUSTRIAL RELATIONS, vol. 10, no. 1, February 1971.*

. . . AND WHAT PROFESSORS THINK: ABOUT STUDENT PROTEST AND MANNERS, MORALS, POLITICS, AND CHAOS ON THE CAMPUS, by Seymour Martin Lipset and Everett C. Ladd, Jr., reprinted from PSYCHOLOGY TODAY, November 1970.*

DEMAND AND SUPPLY IN U.S. HIGHER EDUCATION: A PROGRESS REPORT, by Roy Radner and Leonard S. Miller, reprinted from AMERICAN ECONOMIC REVIEW, May 1970.*

RESOURCES FOR HIGHER EDUCATION: AN ECONOMIST'S VIEW, by Theodore W. Schultz, reprinted from JOURNAL OF POLITICAL ECONOMY, vol. 76, no. 3, University of Chicago, May/June 1968.*

INDUSTRIAL RELATIONS AND UNIVERSITY RELATIONS, by Clark Kerr, reprinted from PROCEEDINGS OF THE 21ST ANNUAL WINTER MEETING OF THE INDUSTRIAL RELATIONS RESEARCH ASSOCIATION, pp. 15–25.*

NEW CHALLENGES TO THE COLLEGE AND UNIVERSITY, by Clark Kerr, reprinted from Kermit Gordon (ed.), AGENDA FOR THE NATION, The Brookings Institution, Washington, D.C., 1968.*

PRESIDENTIAL DISCONTENT, by Clark Kerr, reprinted from David C. Nichols (ed.), PERSPECTIVES ON CAMPUS TENSIONS: PAPERS PREPARED FOR THE SPECIAL COMMITTEE ON CAMPUS TENSIONS, American Council on Education, Washington, D.C., September 1970.*

STUDENT PROTEST—AN INSTITUTIONAL AND NATIONAL PROFILE, by Harold Hodgkinson, reprinted from THE RECORD, vol. 71, no. 4, May 1970.*

WHAT'S BUGGING THE STUDENTS?, by Kenneth Keniston, reprinted from EDUCATIONAL RECORD, American Council on Education, Washington, D.C., Spring 1970.*

THE POLITICS OF ACADEMIA, by Seymour Martin Lipset, reprinted from David C. Nichols (ed.), PERSPECTIVES ON CAMPUS TENSIONS: PAPERS PREPARED FOR THE SPECIAL COMMITTEE ON CAMPUS TENSIONS, American Council on Education, Washington, D.C., September 1970.*

INTERNATIONAL PROGRAMS OF U.S. COLLEGES AND UNIVERSITIES: PRIORITIES FOR THE SEVENTIES, by James A. Perkins, reprinted by permission of the International Council for Educational Development, Occasional Paper no. 1, July 1971.

FACULTY UNIONISM: FROM THEORY TO PRACTICE, by Joseph W. Garbarino, reprinted from INDUSTRIAL RELATIONS, vol. 11, no. 1, pp. 1–17, February 1972.

MORE FOR LESS: HIGHER EDUCATION'S NEW PRIORITY, by Virginia B. Smith, reprinted from UNIVERSAL HIGHER EDUCATION: COSTS AND BENEFITS, American Council on Education, Washington, D.C., 1971.

ACADEMIA AND POLITICS IN AMERICA, by Seymour M. Lipset, reprinted from Thomas J. Nossiter (ed.), IMAGINATION AND PRECISION IN THE SOCIAL SCIENCES, pp. 211–289, Faber and Faber, London, 1972.

POLITICS OF ACADEMIC NATURAL SCIENTISTS AND ENGINEERS, *by Everett C. Ladd, Jr., and Seymour M. Lipset, reprinted from* SCIENCE, *vol. 176, no. 4039, pp. 1091–1100, June 9, 1972.*

THE INTELLECTUAL AS CRITIC AND REBEL: WITH SPECIAL REFERENCE TO THE UNITED STATES AND THE SOVIET UNION, *by Seymour M. Lipset and Richard B. Dobson, reprinted from* DAEDALUS, *vol. 101, no. 3, pp. 137–198, Summer 1972.*

THE POLITICS OF AMERICAN SOCIOLOGISTS, *by Seymour M. Lipset and Everett C. Ladd, Jr., reprinted from* THE AMERICAN JOURNAL OF SOCIOLOGY, *vol. 78, no. 1, July 1972.*

THE DISTRIBUTION OF ACADEMIC TENURE IN AMERICAN HIGHER EDUCATION, *by Martin Trow, reprinted from* THE TENURE DEBATE, *Bardwell Smith (ed.), Jossey-Bass, San Francisco, 1972.*

THE NATURE AND ORIGINS OF THE CARNEGIE COMMISSION ON HIGHER EDUCATION, *by Alan Pifer, reprinted by permission of The Carnegie Foundation for the Advancement of Teaching,* speech delivered Oct. 16, 1972.

COMING OF MIDDLE AGE IN HIGHER EDUCATION, *by Earl F. Cheit, address delivered to American Association of State Colleges and Universities and National Association of State Universities and Land-Grant Colleges, Nov. 13, 1972.*

*The Commission's stock of this reprint has been exhausted.